The Disney College Program 2.0:

An Updated Unofficial and Unauthorized Survival Guide

By: Eric Root

Table of Contents

Note from the Author

Chapter 1: A Very Brief History of the Disney College Program

Chapter 2: The Recruiting Process

Chapter 3: Decisions to Make Before You Arrive

Chapter 4: Getting Around Central Florida

Chapter 5: Time to Check In For the Program!

Chapter 6: Here Comes the Work Fun!

Chapter 7: Time for Fun!

Chapter 8: Your College Program and Relationships

Chapter 9: The Reality of Your Program

Chapter 10: Career Development

Chapter 11: Uh Oh! I Have a Mandatory Housing Meeting!

Chapter 12: Is There Anything Else You Need To Know?

Chapter 13: End of Program

Chapter 14: What Should You Do Next?

Chapter 15: The Top 25 Reasons Why You Should Be A CP

Chapter 16: A Final Few Words

Bonus Section: Further Support

About the Author

Sources

Note from the Author

First off, thank you for taking the time to purchase this book. I have spent many hours compiling the information contained herein. Before you start reading the chapters, please note that this book is not endorsed by or authorized by the Walt Disney Company. I wrote this guide after having left the company. This way you get a realistic perspective from someone who used to work closely with Disney College Program Cast and get solid information and advice from people who were in the exact same spot you are in now. They all had to start from scratch with very little or no real information besides what little info they were able to find on their own. And aren't you looking for information that is realistic and not just fluffed up to just show you that everything is perfect?

Do you have a love or a passion for all things Disney? Maybe you have even had a dream of working for Disney at one point too. Now you are looking at internships and came across this one. Your heart is telling you to go for it. And now you want to be a Disney College Program Cast Member. Well when you look online, you start to realize that there really isn't a lot of information out there besides what the official website says. It is very informative but it doesn't go into very much depth about the realistic side of internships. As I was conducting my interviews with former College Program Cast Members, I was actually surprised that there has never been an unofficial survival guide before now! The little bit of information I was able to find were common descriptions like: a paid internship, housing available to College Program (CP) Cast, transportation available and free admission to the parks. Recruiters on campus will offer the same information but their videos will focus on Cast having fun, a lot of selfie photos of Cast wearing ear hats and people genuinely having a good time. These are all positive and good things that do occur for College Program Cast that complete their program. But where this is nice to build motivation to join, there is a huge drop off in information to really help you through the process and to properly set you up for success.

This book has been written to help the thousands of you deciding on whether or not to join the Disney College Program what to expect and how to be best prepared for your overall program. After having worked in Disney Leadership for over a decade, I learned that many new College Program Cast Members (CPs) did not receive enough initial information to help them adjust to their "internship". I have been compiling information for over a decade from interviewing my CPs outside of work for the sole purpose of creating (what I believe to be) a solid resource to help all CP hopefuls in their journey through the program and at its conclusion. I will also include any source internet websites when I list specifics on pubic viewable policies. The great news here is that the websites are readily accessible and they are free to view by anyone with an internet connection. Please understand that there are some pieces of information that I will not be able to share. Information such as park attendance, trade secrets, specific non-public policies and how attractions are run are off limits. When you join the Walt Disney Company, everyone is required to sign a non-disclosure agreement. This is to protect the company and...quite frankly to preserve the magic. You will learn all kinds of insider information on your own during your program. The information contained within are predominantly concerning the Walt Disney World College Program experience since this is the location I have the most experience with.

So why do I consider myself an expert in this subject matter? Here's a look at my Disney resume: Disney Store leader for two years, hourly Sales host / Core Trainer in Disney's Hollywood Studios theme park for seven months, Mickey's of Hollywood Leader for two years, Tatooine Traders (Backlands Merchandise) Leader for three and a half years, Hollywood Hills Leader for six months and Adventureland Merchandise Leader (Magic Kingdom) for approximately three years. When you do the math, it means I have been with the Walt Disney Company for over a decade! I've not only been in a role governed by union contracts but I have also been actively engaged in Cast training to ensure that the new Cast Members (including CPs) understood the attendance policy.

As you read through this, keep in mind there will be times when the advice I give seems harsh or rough and it will become repetitive. I feel it is extremely important that you have a chance to be set up for better success than if you went into the program completely blind or misinformed. I promise it isn't all doom and gloom. This is just good, sound, practical advice. I will also be including fun things for you to do or consider doing in your down time. For your convenience, I will be including the addresses of these locations so you can use your Smartphone GPS to get there safely.

I truly believe that the Disney College Program is a fantastic experience for anyone who joins as long as they understand what they will have to endure along with enjoy. Many successful leaders with the company started off in the College Program. I have personally worked with some former CPs who are current Disney Leaders. And I have also seen others go onto successful careers with other companies as well. Your Disney experience is an incredibly valuable asset to your future career and endeavors.

In this book, I cover a very brief history of the College Program but mostly the information you need to know now about how to make your College Program successful. Working for Walt Disney World or Disneyland as a CP can be very rewarding and a lot of fun but as you read on, keep in mind it is what it is designed to be: work and work experience. This book is not an official Disney publication but rather a practical guide filled with easy to understand tips and common sense to help you through your program. Again, at no point do I or will I disclose proprietary information or company secrets. Sorry folks. I'm not interested in legal issues. I just want to make sure that you (the reader) have a chance to be set up for success. I have always cared about my Cast and their development. Even though I am no longer with the company, I still care enough to want to help you, the College Program recruit.

I do apologize ahead of time. Again, this book will feel at times repetitive but take comfort in knowing that it is done by design. I have chosen to repeat some items that are great pieces of advice for you to remember as you embark on the journey known as: The Disney College Program!

Best of luck in your pursuit of a successful Disney College Program Internship,

Eric Root

Chapter 1
A Very Brief History of the Disney College Program

In the Beginning

On July 17, 1955, The Disneyland theme park opened in Anaheim, CA. The park became extremely successful thanks to the brilliance of Walt Disney and his brother Roy. But as the story goes, there came a point where the brothers were disappointed that they weren't able to expand like they wanted to. Hotels and other attractions quickly sprang up and surrounded the theme park in no time. When Walt Disney passed away on December 15th, 1966, his Florida Project was on hold. His brother Roy decided to continue the project but name the location Walt Disney World in honor of his brother. So after careful planning and many years of maneuvering, the Disney Company expanded to Central Florida by opening up the Magic Kingdom theme park on October 1st, 1971. Since the company was able to acquire so much more land, it left open the possibilities of future expansion that Anaheim's site has never had the luxury of. The popularity of Florida theme park was prevalent and soon after, the company planned on building part of Walt's original dream of E.P.C.O.T. (Experimental Prototype Community of Tomorrow) Center. Walt's original dream wasn't completely possible because to make EPCOT, it would have required the location to become its own government entity and the Disney company would no longer be a business. Or so that is at least how one of the stories goes for what it's worth.

Then the College Program Forms

Guests flocked to the Magic Kingdom since the only other close Disney park was over three thousand miles away. This type of patronage meant that growth would be inevitable. And with growth would eventually come more jobs to Central Florida. But during these early years of the Disney Parks in Central Florida, there wasn't a college program available for college students to apply. There was none available either in the Anaheim park. The College Program actually didn't come in to fruition until 1981. It was a modest program in the beginning to say the least. At the start, there were only a few hundred students who were able to work in Magic Kingdom. Since Magic Kingdom was the only park available at the time, there wasn't a large demand. But those first few hundred Cast Members were actually a part of the Magic Kingdom College Program. This was the only park available and the resort only had a couple of hotels at this time. So again opportunities were very limited. But eventually word got out that a program existed and applications begin flying in to the Casting Office in spite of the lack of positions available. As thousands of applications came in, there were still only a few hundred CP roles available. These pioneer CPs were a part of a really exclusive alumni once they completed their program. As Epcot opened to the public on October 1st, 1982, the program grew to accommodate a few hundred more students. In the early stages of the two park program, the name changed from the Magic Kingdom College Program to The Walt Disney World College Program. A few hundred College Program positions then became several hundred and the applications also doubled. But with this growth came a need to house these CPs. Fun Fact: The oldest current College Program Housing, Vista Way Apartments didn't come into use until 1987.

CPs Need Housing Too!

Before then, College Program Cast stayed in an off property mobile home park. Once Vista Way became available, Cast were placed closer to their work locations. This made it easier and more efficient to get the Cast to work in a timely manner. But there wasn't any more room to expand the program. Two theme parks and a couple of resorts still do not boast enough opportunity for college students or grads to experience the joys of the program yet. Then Walt Disney World resort began adding additional theme parks Disney's Hollywood Studios (then Disney MGM-Studios) in 1989 and Disney's Animal Kingdom in April of 1998. The opportunities grew into the thousands now. More and more resorts were being built to accommodate Guests and the ever growing crowds that frequented the properties. Disneyland joined the program and began recruiting College Program candidates in 2004. Also, incredible expansion in the form of water parks, Downtown Disney (Soon to be Disney Springs) and resorts flourished through the 1990's and 2000's.

With Expansion Comes Opportunity

With this fast growth also came new opportunities to recruit even more College Program Cast Members. Think of it like this: the more a business grows the more positions that become available! Now the Disney College Program recruits thousands of college students and grads throughout the year on both coasts. Disneyland is much smaller and has (currently) only the two theme parks and three resorts in addition to Downtown Disney. This means that here are a lot less positions available for the Anaheim location than the Central Florida resort.

According to an article in the Orlando Sentinel on January 30, 2015 by Sandra Pedicini, Walt Disney World brings in more than 12,000 new College Program recruits each year! Now this may sound like a lot but keep in mind, more than 50,000 people apply. Not everyone makes it through the initial screening process. All Cast need to pass a background check. And if you have legal issues in your past including anything that includes a felony, you may want to save yourself some embarrassment and skip the application process. If you have no major past issues, you could be one of those 12,000 if you put your mind to it! Want to read the article? You can read it here at this website:
http://www.orlandosentinel.com/business/tourism/os-disney-college-program-20150130-story.html

The more positions available in the College Program means that more and more housing locations are needed to accommodate the incoming Cast. As of this publication, the current College Program Housing locations are: Vista Way, Chatham Square, The Commons, and Patterson Court. Please note that other apartment complexes can be added and subtracted based on the amount of College Program participants.

Recently, the Walt Disney Company announced that there are major expansions on the horizon! Disney's Animal Kingdom is still scheduled for an expansion involving James Cameron's film: Avatar. Disney's Hollywood Studios (which may or may not go through a name change in the future) has announced to the public that there are additions coming to that park as well. A larger Star Wars and Indiana Jones presence in the park are possibly on the way. Once these offerings go live (plus any other projects the company works on and completes) means that there could be more opportunities for people like yourself in the College Program! These are very exciting times indeed!

Is that all, you ask? Well I did say it would be a brief history of the College Program!

Chapter 2
The Recruiting Process

How did you first learn about the Disney College Program? In order to be involved or to try and apply for the Disney College Program, you will need to be a part of the recruiting process in some capacity. The recruiting process typically involves CP Campus representatives coming to your local campus and holding expos at various times of the year. College Program typically begins for new hires in the spring and fall. The expos tend to take place well before these start times to allow the recruiters time to get candidates through the process. The nice thing about having College Program campus representatives on your campus is that they tend to be College Program Alumni. And the odds are high that they were also or are also a current student at you college or university. This means that at one point in their Disney career, they were in your shoes! Well not literally though I'm sure your shoes are quite lovely. This makes them a great resource if you ask the right questions. Please remember that they have a goal. Their goal is to fill a quota of a specified number of spots for the upcoming college program.

Beyond the Campus Reps

Those without campus reps or expos, end up finding out about the program through word-of-mouth and by finding the program on the Disney website. Word-of-mouth can be very valuable since you are able to get first hand information from someone who has been through the program. Hopefully their program was fairly recent so you aren't left with simple statements like: "It was so much fun" or "It was the best experience ever." These statements are nice but they aren't very informative or helpful. Someone who has recently completed the program will give you their perspective on the positives and negatives. Keep in mind that if you ask various College Program alumni about their experience, you will get varying degrees in their answers. There is no such thing as a cookie cutter experience. Each person experiences their own journey and own growth. But at least you are able to gain some much needed perspective. On a side note: some of the CPs I interviewed did say that their campus representative did properly fill them in on what they will endure during their program. Some recruiters even offered ample time for a questions and answers session to help you in your decision process.

Regardless of how a candidate discovers the program, they will need to visit the website, fill out a questionnaire and answer a series of questions to determine their level of honesty and integrity. Understand that the questions asked in this process are asking you how you conduct yourself in a business environment. This screening process is used to determine whether Disney is willing to bring a candidate into the program. If a candidate happens to get a response stating that they are not eligible for the program at this time, they will have to wait six (6) months before attempting the application process again. You can visit the website by typing this into your web browser: **http://cp.disneycareers.com/en/default/**

For those that move on to an email of acceptance in the program will need to log on to their profile account and select their preferences. Some receive a phone interview that covers this process instead. You will be asked to pick what line of business to work in. Please note: it is just the line of business and NOT where you want to work. Recruiters have a quota to fill for specific lines of business. High demand roles are food & Beverage, Merchandise, Custodial, Attractions and Transportation / Parking. So if you happen to select Operations as a choice, there is a distinct possibility that you could end up working in Custodial, Attractions or Main Entrance. All of these are classified under the Operations line of business. Unfortunately, you most likely won't have a choice to choose between them since it is all based on which area needs the most assistance. I mention this again only because my former CPs have all stated the same thing: the recruiter is high energy and will show you a lot of fun photos. In order to get true information, it is up to you to ask questions. You need to understand the big picture before jumping into the program. Set yourself up for success!

International College Program Cast also goes through a similar recruiting process. International College Program start times vary based on the work visas they are issued. The time they are allotted to stay in the program is based on the work Visa they are issued. International College Program Cast working in World Showcase (more often than not) tends to have a work Visa for an entire year. It has been my experience that most ICPs have anywhere between two months and six months on their program. The program is typically split into halves and the Cast Member works in two different locations sometimes even two different lines of business. Since work Visas are very limiting in what an International College Program Cast Member are able to do, once they are selected for a role or roles, they are stuck there for the duration of their program.

There are some roles that United States based College Program Cast Members will not be eligible for. Lines of business like attractions maintenance, food and beverage (restaurants) in World Showcase and stage techs are typically not available through regular College Program recruiting. These roles are considered advanced technical roles. Most require some type of certification through the state and have Full and Part Time Cast Members that have extensive training. The World Showcase contains restaurants that are third party operated and also require the staff to be from those specific countries like China, Japan and Germany to name a few.

Just be sure that you really think about where you want to work. Understanding that the Magic Kingdom tends to be the park with the longest hours but also means that it is the park with more opportunities. These opportunities give you a chance to be a part of the magic! If you try to avoid areas you consider busy, you could be limiting yourself to future career growth if you have a dream of working for Disney as a long term career.

Will I get College Credit?

College credit for your internship would be an added bonus for you participating! But to find the correct answer to this question, you will need to check with your campus representative or with your school administration if you found the program online without the help of a college recruiter. Every school is different. And those that do give any kind of credit will most likely have specific requirements that or benchmarks that you will need to achieve in order for them to take your College Program seriously. Be sure to ask questions and ask for any requirements they might have in writing. This will help you use the requirements as a checklist or guideline as you are actively involved in your program. You might be relying on your Disney leadership team or required CP classes to assist you with proving that you finished your college campus' requirements.

What Roles Are Potentially Available?

In California and Florida, the following lines of business tend to be recruiting for the College Program:
· Operations
· Entertainment
· Lodging
· Food & Beverage
· Retail / Sales
· Recreation

Within in each of these categories, there are subcategories to consider as well!
· Operations in California - Attractions, Custodial, Transportation & Parking, Park Photographers and Park Greeters
· Operations in Florida - Attractions, Custodial, Park Photographers, Main Entrance Operations and Transportation
· Entertainment in California - Cast Costuming and Entertainment Costuming
· Entertainment in Florida - Character Attendant and Costuming.

Do you have dreams of being a Disney Princess or maybe one of your favorite characters from animated features? Well if you want to be a performer, you must audition! Understand that auditions can be extremely disappointing for many people. You could go to the audition and completely nail whatever dance or walk they ask of you and STILL be denied. But why did this happen to you? Was it because you wore the wrong colored socks with your sandals? First off, why are you wearing socks with sandals? You may want to rethink your wardrobe strategy. But realistically it was because they just weren't looking for your specific height and build right at that moment. Auditions are done for business need purposes. When there is a need for a specific height and build, auditions take place. Just don't let a denial make you sad or angry. Remember that many people have the same dream as you. They also want to be a character. Make sure you study up on what range of character you qualify for. I'm a six foot three inch large man that has facial hair and wears a fedora. I knew they would never slap fairy wings on me and push me out of the Castle window. I'm realistic like that. And make sure you stick to the guidelines of what is required. As I would tell some of my Cast that had their own creative ideas if they became a character, "Just because you ARE a character doesn't mean you will get picked to BE a character." Improvisations are typically frowned upon in order to maintain the integrity of a character's persona with Guests and the overall public. Check back for the next audition dates and try again! For more information on auditioning, visit the website at: **https://disneyprogramsblog.com/disney-college-program-auditions/**

- Lodging in California - Disney Desk, Front Desk and Guest Services
- Lodging in Florida - Bell Services, Concierge, Hospitality and Housekeeping
- Food & Beverage in California - Custodial Busser, Cart Cashier, Food Prep, Quick Service Cashier and Quick Service Restaurant host / hostess
- Food & Beverage in Florida - Full Service (non-tipped) and Quick Service (non-tipped)

- Retail / Sales in California - Retail Sales Clerk & Vacation Planner
- Retail / Sales in Florida - Floral, Merchandise, Vacation Planner, Fairy Godmother at Bibbity Bobbity Boutique and Pirate Master at the Pirate's League
- Recreation in California - Lifeguard
- Recreation in Florida - Lifeguard and Recreation

As you can see there are quite a few choices of roles you can do. But here is where you need to choose carefully. What is your overall goal? Are you looking for a career? Or are you just there for the experience? Certain areas are career limited just because of the nature of the businesses. There are traditionally more long term opportunities when you choose a role that has locations spread out all over property. For example: Merchandise, Operations and Food and Beverage are everywhere. They contain more roles and tend to have more opportunities for advancement or even lateral transfers when desired. Working in locations like: Bibbity Bobbity Boutique and The Pirate's League are very limited in the number of overall positions available and are also extremely limited in advancement since there are only a couple of roles higher than what you start at. The experiences that each of these locations give are memorable but can potentially be confining since the locations are small. If you are claustrophobic or have issues with crowded rooms, these locations might not be a right fit for you. Just consider yourself warned.

Also, you can consider this as well: If you successfully complete the Disney College Program and you still have school left to finish, you might have the opportunity to become a campus representative! Then you have the opportunity to recruit others into the College Program. There are a few perks of being a campus representative while you finish your degree. Look at you! A possible recruiter someday! Okay but let's not put the cart before the horse (so to speak). You haven't even worked a single shift yet as a CP intern.

Now that you have signed up for the College Program, you have some planning to do!

Chapter 3
Decisions to Make Before You Arrive

By now you can hardly contain your excitement! You might even be watching your entire Disney movie collection in anticipation of you being a part of the magic. It's okay if you do. Nobody will judge you. I too have an extensive Disney movie collection. Fun Fact: My favorite Disney Animated film is Alice in Wonderland. I don't know why but I just like the fact that it is nonsense. Oh and Marvel and Star Wars films count as a part of your Disney Movie Collection since they own the franchises. Okay, I digress. So you've seen the online videos, read the blogs and now you're excited to have signed up for the program! Or maybe you haven't found any blogs that give you real answers to the questions you have had about the program in general. Well you have taken a solid step forward in learning more by reading this book. Since you have already signed up, now you have some serious decisions to make.

Choose Your Transportation Wisely

Everyone needs transportation in Orlando. But how will you be getting around Disney property or even Orlando? Will you be bringing a car to your program or will you be relying on Disney transportation to get you around? Your transportation choices are very important! Some people like the freedom of being able to sleep in before coming to work. I know I was quite fond of being able to leave work at the end of my day and heading straight to my car. Once I was on the road, I was home in about fifteen to twenty minutes depending on traffic. Others like the peaceful ride of a bus while listening to their favorite music on their earbuds or headphones. The music helps while you are not only waiting for the correct College Program bus but also the various stops your bus might make before dropping you off out front of your Housing Complex.

How Will You Pay For Your Rent?

Rent payments or housing payments in general are typically inescapable. In order to live in an apartment as an adult, you will need to pay rent. Being on the Disney College Program is no different. But you will need to decide on an option of payment if you are offered more than one. Will you be placing a credit card on file with your housing to pay for rent? Or will you have your rent deducted from your weekly paycheck at Disney? Maybe your program won't give you any other options than one or another? Apartment living as an adult also means making sure that your rent is paid per your rental agreement. Remember that being in this program means that paying your rent on time is your only option. This apartment situation is different than anything out in the "real world".

To answer these questions, you must ask yourself; do I plan on joining the program for a vacation or to actually get work experience out of it? If your answer involves the word "vacation", you will most likely want to set up your rent to be paid via credit card. The reason for this is that you will probably be giving away shifts, calling out on scheduled days and most likely won't work enough hours to pay your rent through payroll. Oh and you will most likely get termed since you will accrue too many points and fail your program. But hey! You just had one heck of a vacation. Right? Wrong! This is a horrible way to think of your program and will only end up backfiring on you. Sorry to blunt about this but this happens more often than not. I will cover more on this scenario in a bit.

By setting up through payroll deductions, this will force you to budget your money which is also a handy skill set for the future. Regardless of which decision you make on payment, just understand that your rent is deducted weekly just as you are paid weekly. Being paid weekly definitely has its advantages! Since the rules of the College Program are subject to change before each program, there is a chance that you might only have one option to pay your rent. Just be sure you are ready to comply with whatever option is made available to you.

The amount of rent you will pay is determined by how many roommates you are assigned and which apartment complex you are assigned to. The more roommates you have, the less your rent. The less of an amount of roommates you have, the more the rent is per person. But do understand that the amount of rent you are charged is still quite high. But look on the bright side. Your apartment is fully furnished! Though you will be sharing bathroom space as well so make sure you plan ahead for your scheduled day. Yes, the housing office does have the apartment and furniture cleaned after apartments are vacated. So, there is no need to worry or fret over someone else's cooties. The reason for this is that transportation is offered to you on your program. Whether you utilize it or not, it has to be paid for by some means.

Leave the Valuable Belongings Back Home

Everyone has at least one personal belonging that we cherish. It may have real value or maybe only sentimental value. I highly suggest that you do not bring items of extreme value or sentimental value that you would be devastated if it became lost or broken. Although new CPs go through the same recruitment process and background check, your roommates are people who come from all various locations and backgrounds. Now I don't think you were planning on coming to your program with millions of dollars in diamonds and furs. Besides, furs are a ridiculous thing to even consider in this hot tropical environment and do you really want to be wearing dead animals anyways? But in any case, sometimes good people are tempted by opportunity. Lockers are assigned to you and are subject to random housing inspections. Now I understand that you can't live without your Playstation or X-Box but just exercise caution. When you are not at home, you don't know who might be hanging out in your apartment. Ultimately you can do what you like but just think about what I've just stated for a moment.

Like to Get Your Party On?

You are off of work and it is time to let loose! But hold on just a second there. If you are in an apartment that is under 21 or considered a "wellness" apartment, don't plan on sneaking anything with liquor into the apartment. Anyone under the age of 21 caught consuming, buying or supplying liquor to under the age of 21 will not only be terminated but will most likely be facing legal charges as well. Know the law. There will be times that maybe you and your roommates want to throw a party or maybe you were invited to a party at somebody else's apartment. You have to remember that you live in an apartment complex. You have neighbors (albeit Cast Members) and your neighbors have different working shifts than you. Don't let your partying get out of control or too loud. Make sure you follow your housing guidelines on noise levels and time of day. You are responsible for your guests and if they get out of hand at your party, it could result in a negative situation for you. If you are old enough to drink alcohol legally, please drink responsibly! This mess is easily avoidable if you act accordingly.

But How Should You Dress While on Your Program?

Pack appropriate clothing! You will most likely be issued costumes for work but don't forget to pack weather appropriate clothes for your down time. You will also need to pack some professional attire as well. The first few days are training and classes at Disney University. You will want to make sure that you have some professional wear for any tours that you are to go on such as the tour new Cast get at the four parks, Downtown Disney and the resorts. Looking your best along with a smile goes far for first impressions and also in case you are approached by a Guest.

Depending on when your program is, understand that Florida is warm except for about 2-3 months out of the year. Unless you are from a tropical climate, warm in Florida is different from warm in places like Texas, New York, Nebraska or even Georgia. January through early March can see temperatures range from 60 to 75. It can get very cold (30 to 40 degrees) during this time as well. March and April see temps around 75 to 85 but comfortable usually. The real heat and humidity sets in around May through September and even as late as October or November. Fortunately, all of the apartments, shops and indoor attractions have air conditioning but please make sure to remember to hydrate, hydrate, and hydrate! Water is the only way to stay properly hydrated. Disney leaders and Safety modules state this early and often. Dehydration is easily avoidable as long as you are consuming a lot of water throughout your day. Remember: if you are thirsty, you are already showing signs of dehydration. Carbonated sugar beverages are not helpful for hydration. They actually dehydrate you quicker.

Anaheim, CA has a calmer climate. It gets warm in summer and cold in the winter. The spring and fall climates are quite nice minus the days of rain they experience. It is much different than the Florida weather but you will still need to remember to stay hydrated either way!

Be Flexible!

You can budget and still plan on having fun! There are plenty of things to do that won't break the bank. You just need to be mindful of your finances. Now if you happen to have a trust fund or wealthy family members, congratulations! You are a possible minority amongst CPs so spend away! The sky's the limit! Just kidding! Don't spend away. You should still understand how basic economics work and should plan on budgeting to live within your means. Wealthy people don't stay wealthy by blowing through their fortune. Consider that a life lesson.

If your apartment happens to lose a roommate or two, you could be subjected to a new roommate being added or the remaining roommates being relocated into a new apartment. Why would this happen? You could lose a roommate or two for various reasons. Maybe a roommate was so home sick that they decided that being away from home is not for them. You could lose a roommate if they rack up too many attendance points and they were let go and marked as a non-complete for their program. If a roommate quits just because and they vacate your apartment, keep in mind that there are many different reasons but it could mean that the remaining roommates will be subject to change in the overall household. Just be positive and remain flexible. Not everybody is fond of change but it is a potential reality. If you are required to move within a specified period of time, make sure you call your leadership team or Cast Deployment and communicate with them what is going on. They will work with you as best as possible. Your leadership team understands that there are possible times that College Program Housing will have mandatory requirements of you. Keeping your team in the loop with good proactive communication is the key to going through these situations smoothly.

Chapter 4
Getting Around Central Florida

Will You Bring a Car?

If you have chosen to drive to Walt Disney World for your program, you will come into contact with the dreaded Interstate 4 (or I-4) freeway. It is heavily traveled by tourists and locals every day. It can be extremely painful and long to drive between exits 60 and 72 since this is a heavy tourist area. Walt Disney World, Universal Studios Orlando and Sea World exits are located in this stretch. Each day this major freeway has bumper to bumper traffic during the morning rush hour commute and the evening rush hour commute. Since this freeway is heavily traveled to get to the various Central Florida theme parks, traffic congestion stretches into the weekends and daily as the theme parks close. With an updated GPS device or Smartphone, it can be avoided but your travel time might increase since you have ventured off the direct routes. When at all possible do use your GPS. It can be a real life saver if you are new to Orlando or any of the surrounding suburbs. Regardless of which way you go, allow enough extra travel time to reach your destination. Fortunately, there are enough alternate routes and back entrances onto Disney property that will help you tremendously once you know where your work location will be. During special events such as: hard ticket park events, marathons and holidays, the company will issue special alerts for Cast to inform you of any road closures and alternate routes.

Unfortunately, the public transportation service (Lynx buses) is not reliable enough for you to use on your College Program. Their pickup and drop off times and locations are not structured for your needs and also can be a problem for newer full time and part time Cast as well. It really is recommended to have your own vehicle if possible but then you still have to deal with construction on the roads. Construction also seems to be a never ending season in Central Florida as well. With the constant yearly increase in visitors to the sunshine state, the Florida Department of Transportation is constantly working on projects to improve the infrastructure. The roads are constantly being expanded and current roads are being repaired which can sometimes turn into a bit of a commuting nightmare.

You Can Always Use the Disney CP Transportation

But right now you are saying to yourself, "I don't own or have a car." This is not a problem for you on the Disney College Program. You are not required to bring a car with you to your program. So if you are choosing to rely on Disney transportation, it is imperative that you learn the bus system. The buses that CPs use have designated pickups and drop offs. They are coded with a specific lettering and numbering system. Knowing the corresponding letters of the bus, the pickup times and how long it takes on a standard traffic day to get your work location are vital to you. Being late has its consequences and knowing which bus you rode on and the time it should have picked you up will be valuable information to you when communicating with your leaders about transportation issues. Now if driving your own car or taking a Disney bus becomes too cumbersome, you have some alternative transportation choices at your disposal. This will also save you on gassing up your own vehicle and the wear and tear.

Taxi Anyone?

So what is alternative transportation? If you were fortunate to befriend a Cast Member with a car, you could offer to pay for some gas in return for lifts. Keep in mind that if you do this often, you could end up causing your new found friendship status with this Cast Member to be strained. Remember they have a work schedule and a life too! But there are still other options available! Other options include: taxis, shuttles and cars for hire are all legal forms of transportation in Central Florida. **Mears taxi** is the official taxi on property and is one of the biggest in Central Florida. They also tend to be a bit higher in cost of the options but you can call a cab at **407-699-9999** (yellow cab). They also have their own app that will allow you to request a taxi pick up too!

Car for Hire Services

Uber has come onto the scene in Central Florida and has turned into one of the better priced alternatives. Their entrance into the car for hire business has been rocky to start, their service has been impeccable but the true drama has come in the battle with taxi and limos over licensing and vetting of drivers. Fortunately, Orlando came with an agreement with the company as long as its drivers follow specific rules that are set by the city. So you can hail an Uber car from the Uber app if you have a smartphone. Never used Uber before? Use this promo code to get your first ride free (up to $20): **KXU8S** just beware of "surge pricing". This occurs when demand for drivers is high and not enough vehicles are available at the moment. The app will warn you before you it hails a driver. This gives you a chance to decide whether or not you want to pay extra for the service. I am grateful that there are alternatives to a traditional taxi.

Lyft has also become a popular alternative for hiring a car. They also have an app that allows you to hail a driver. Lyft also suffered from initial backlash in the heated debate over car for hire services. They too have a code for your first ride free: **ERIC370703** and yes this is a referral code. But hey! A free ride is a free ride. Both Uber and Lyft are typically the least expensive way to get around Central Florida if you do not have your own car. Both referral codes are valid anywhere that Uber and Lyft are available. Not just Central Florida.

Toll Road Advice

Toll roads are all around Central Florida. You should consider acquiring a Sunpass if you have your own car and plan on traveling to the Atlantic Coast, Kennedy Space Center, Port Canaveral or even the Orlando International Airport. The quickest routes to these places will take you onto a toll road at some point. Now you can do the old fashioned way of paying for your tolls with exact change. However, if you purchase and setup a Sunpass, you can save some money on tolls. And you can drive through specific toll areas and have your toll captured electronically as opposed to waiting in long lines to pay a toll cashier or wait as the cars in front of you scramble to find the exact change they need. Not a lot of money but some money is better than money right? Sunpass is sold at all major retailers and some gas stations. Prices vary on the passes based on the type of unit you buy. You must log onto their website to setup payment. Instructions are included in the packaging with the device.

Want more information on Sunpass? Go to: https://www.sunpass.com/index

Chapter 5
Time to Check In For the Program!

You've Arrived!

Wow! What an exhausting trip! I imagine you have spent the last several hours and days going over a real and virtual checklist of everything you had to remember to complete before you left home. And maybe you even got reminders from family and or friends about what you need to do. Don't look now but you've made it safely to Florida! Whether you came by bus, train, airplane, automobile or walking (not recommended without an amazing pair of comfortable shoes), it is time for you to be a part of the Disney College Program. As of publication time, you will need to make your way to Vista Way. Vista Way is one of a few College Program apartment complexes that house CPs. The address for **Vista Way** is: **13501 Meadow Creek Dr, Orlando, FL 32821** (in case you need to use your GPS or Smartphone to find it) and their current contact number is: **(407) 827-1225**. Try to arrive early if you can. You will be spending literally all day here getting through the check in process the later you arrive.

If you have happened to come across one of the many blogger sites or Facebook pages that pop up concerning College Program or CP Roommates, you can try networking there and meet people to potentially become roommates with. This will help expedite parts of your check in process. Otherwise, you will be waiting with thousands of others to find out which apartment complex and apartment number you will be assigned to once check ins have concluded. Though it would be nice to be able to meet and pre-screen your roommates. Sometimes this method is effective. Just keep an open mind about who you will be sharing your dwelling with.

First Thing You Need to Do Is...

It is now time to check in for your program! You're so excited that you have become nervous. The tall coffee you bought from Starbucks isn't helping you settle down either. Just take a deep breath. Your journey begins...NOW! So what happens during your College Program check in? First, you will have to go solo over to the orientation. Sorry family members are not allowed in. The reason for this is that there are thousands of soon-to-be Cast Members all waiting to get inside for this orientation presentation. If you didn't arrive early, you will be waiting outside for some time until you are able to safely enter the facility. I recommend bringing a bottle of water and maybe a snack in addition to a book or headphones to pass the time. Though you will probably be so excited to be there that you will spend the duration of time meeting the people in line with you. It's never too early to make new friends! The video presentation isn't extremely long but a requirement of all new College Program Cast. It may even be a similar video that you watched on campus that your campus rep showed you. It may not. Everyone's journey to this point seems to be somewhat unique. Pay attention and follow the directions of your facilitator. They should be directing you to the next step.

Fill Out Your New Hire Information

After the orientation is over, you will proceed to a computer station to begin filling out your new hire paperwork. Don't worry if you have to wait for an available computer. Enjoy this process and try not to rush through it. There really is no need for silly mistakes to happen if you are in a hurry. This is an important part of the process since it will also be paperwork that involves getting you paid properly. Read over everything thoroughly and proofread your work. Typing errors can be a pain to fix. Accuracy is important especially when it comes to your pay and taxes withheld. Verify that your home address and social security number are accurate! Sometimes the company will mail you time sensitive materials like: Holiday coupon packets or information about your program. If your mailing address is incorrect, you will not receive these materials and replacing them has become a non-existent option.

Direct Deposit of your check is definitely preferred! If you have a bank that you use normally, great! If they are located in Florida near work, even better! If you don't have a bank, you might run into some issues. As of publication, you can sign to have your payroll deposited into a prepaid Visa. This can be painful though since some banks charge fees for withdrawals. Disney does have its own credit union. Partners Federal Credit Union has a branch at Disney University (behind Magic Kingdom). There is a branch on International Drive close to CP housing. There is a branch inside Team Disney which is across from Downtown Disney. And there are also Partners ATMs scattered across property including in the parks (backstage) and at select resorts. This is a nice option since you can bank normally and are eligible to join as a Cast Member. Just make sure you have a plan. I'm not sure that a paper check is a viable option for College Program anymore. And who wants the hassle of having to travel to a check cashing place after a long day of work and a long bus ride back to your apartment?

Time to Get Your Roommate Assignment!

After your paperwork has concluded, you will have spent anywhere from two to six hours going through to this point. You are next given your housing and roommate assignments. Since this first day is considered move in day, you and your family (if they came with you) can head on over to your assigned apartment complex. You will need to show your housing issued ID (you are assigned the ID card during the check in process) and any family with you will need to present a legal photo ID (Driver's License, Passport or State issued ID). The family will not be allowed to stay on property overnight. They are just allowed to visit during specific hours. Fun Fact: if you have a car with you and are thinking about sneaking somebody into your complex via the trunk of your car, don't. College Program Housing has twenty fur hour security surveillance and they have the right to search your car before they let you through the gate to your apartment complex. You've been warned.

Please understand that even though Vista Way is the oldest of the College Program Housing, it is still painted and maintained. Just like any other apartment complex, repairs and maintenance requests are processed in a timely manner. Yes, if you happen to be sent to Chatham Square or even The Commons, they look nicer and newer. In part because they are! They are newer complexes that were built with a more modern look. Vista Way unfortunately has a bit of a negative reputation for being a party location. Honestly, don't believe all of the hype. Apartments are apartments. How you perceive it is based on how others treat it. If your roommates treat your apartment like a sorority or a frat house, then it will become one. And you will also probably have several run ins with security, housing and other tenants. This behavior could also lead to termination of the program of all individuals in the apartment. Everyone living there is over the age of eighteen at least. If you want the world to treat you like a responsible adult, now is a great time to start acting like one!

For Goodness Sake Go Unpack Your Stuff!

You may have just spent several hours getting checked in and now you might be feeling a little tired. The anxiety of the process is fading. But hang in there! You will need a second wind now because it is time to head on over to your assigned apartment and meet your roommates! Everyone in your apartment is just as nervous as you are and just as anxious to be a part of the magic. This is going to be your new home for at least a few months if not longer. The sooner you settle in, the easier the transition. You will have to work out amongst yourselves as to who sleeps in which bed in which room but you're all adults. You should be able to work this out. While you get to know your roommates, you will want to settle in and unpack. Utilize the assigned locker you are given for valuables. Do not forget to stop and eat something or at least eat a snack! Hours will click by quickly if you aren't careful. You will want to remember to drink water and stay hydrated but also take time to eat something. Everyone is responsible for purchasing their own foods and toiletries. Remember this isn't a vacation or summer camp. Be respectful and courteous to others and their personal space especially in the beginning. You probably do not know these people very well and it would be awkward to assume that everyone will be best friends by the end of their program. It could happen but it could also not.

Your First Run To the Grocery Store

Oh no! You didn't pack any sundries because you flew in? Or maybe you just forgot to pick some up on the drive in? Don't worry! You won't need to ask your new roommates to borrow their deodorant. Besides, that's just gross! Also, even though your apartment is furnished, you still need items like toilet paper, paper towels, food, shampoo, towels, linens, a pillow, snacks and anything else you would typically have available to yourself in your own home. These items are not supplied for you unfortunately. Fortunately, there are some grocery stores close by for you to go grab the products you will need to use or food to eat. To get there, you still have an option to take the College Program bus to the local grocery store. Keep in mind this is the option that could take the longest since the buses run on schedules. You could drive to one of a few different places to buy groceries. This is the quickest option since you have the freedom to drive where you want and when you want. There is also the taxi, Uber or Lyft options if you want to get there and back quicker than the buses.

For your convenience, I have included the names of current local grocery stores and their addresses for you if you are driving or taking a car for hire service:

Wal-Mart Supercenter: 3250 Vineland Rd, Kissimmee, FL 34746 (located close to Vista Way)
Target (SuperTarget): 4795 W Irlo Bronson Memorial Hwy, Kissimmee, FL 34746-5332
Publix Grocery Store: 8145 Vineland Ave Orlando, FL 32821-6847 (located close to Chatham Square, the Commons and Mickey's Retreat area)
Publix Grocery Store: 2915 Vineland Rd Kissimmee, FL 34746-5505 (located closer to Vista Way than the other CP Housing)

Keep in mind that there are other places to buy groceries as well but these just happen to be the closest. I tend to coupon and BOGO shop (buy one get one) so I gravitate towards these locations a lot. At least it's something you should consider since your money isn't unlimited. And if you are a rare one percent person where money is no object, congratulations! But for the other ninety nine percent, don't be afraid to ad shop these stores online. All stores in the area are going to be busy regardless of which one you choose. This entire geographical area is one big tourist location so you will be shopping with locals and tourists alike. Just be patient and take your time.

Have Medical Needs?

Medical issues can arise as a part of everyday life. If you have insurance through your family, check the insurance website for possible in-network primary care physicians. It is always good to be prepared. Most insurance companies will allow you to switch between primary care physicians and back once you go home. There are PLENTY of pharmacies in and around the area. Center for Living Well is located in the Epcot Cast Services Parking Lot. They are currently affiliated with Florida Hospital and accept new patients if you make them your primary care. They also have a pharmacy inside that is currently operated by Walgreens. Whatever you do, don't neglect your medical needs if any. Emergency rooms and Urgent Care can be costly in their co-pay requirements. It is a good idea to bring any initial medications with you that you might need from home before you arrive. You can always research which pharmacies will honor your refill prescriptions. But most importantly, this will also buy you time if you need to have your primary care from back home write you a prescription that they can fax to a local pharmacy here if you need it. Wait times will vary from day to day even with an appointment so just be patient (so to speak).

There are also a couple of hospitals and urgent care clinics close by:
- Celebration Hospital - 400 Celebration Pl, Kissimmee, FL 34747 (open 24 hours)

- Lake Buena Vista Centra Care - 12500 S Apopka Vineland Rd, Orlando, FL 32836 (hours vary)
- Doctor P. Phillips Hospital - 9400 Turkey Lake Rd, Orlando, FL 32819
- Florida Hospital Kissimmee - 2450 N Orange Blossom Trail, Kissimmee, FL 34744

There are others but these are the ones closest to College Program Housing.

Do you suffer from food allergies? The restaurants on Disney property and many off property take food allergies very seriously. You should consult your server if you do have a food allergy issue. The Chefs are trained to consult you and offer you alternative dishes to accommodate your allergen needs. Just be aware that Central Florida has hundreds of buffet style restaurants in and around the area. My advice to those with food allergies is to skip these locations. It is too easy to come across cross contaminated foods since the food is handled directly by patrons consuming the product.

Need Fuel For Your Car?

In the state of Florida, you will be pumping your own gas. My condolences go out to residents of state like Oregon where pumping your own gas is illegal. While you are in Florida you will become a gas pumping expert. But just as a warning to you: the gas station right next to Vista Way is one of the most expensive in the area. It is in the heart of a tourist trap and unfortunately, a lot of CPs use it due to convenience. The gas stations on Disney Property are less expensive than that place. Other gas stations close by to the complexes as of publication: on Highway 535: Wawa (near the Vista Way Wal-Mart), Racetrack (near both Vista Way , Chatham and the Commons). There are others around but these tend to have better pricing than others. Please feel free to shop around. The gas stations on Highway 535 between Vista Way and an area called The Crossroads (near Hotel Plaza Boulevard on Disney property) tend to have some of the highest fuel prices. Again, it is a heavily traveled tourist area. Traveling further away from this area will you give a better value for money.

There are two gas stations (currently) on Disney property as well for convenience. One is located by Magic Kingdom and one is located near Downtown Disney (soon to be Disney Spring). The location by Magic Kingdom also has a AAA Car Care Center there as well. So if you have AAA and have car issues, you can take comfort in knowing that help is really close to work and home! There are also a couple of rental car businesses on Disney property if you find the need to rent a car and go out of town on your days off. Prices for rentals are subject to change and you will need to see if you qualify to rent a car based on your age and insurability.

Staying at Chatham Square or the Commons? Have access to no vehicle but want to go shopping? How about a walk over to the Outlet Mall! The Orlando Vineland Premium Outlets® is located at 8200 Vineland Avenue, Orlando, FL 32821 and are accessible by foot through the housing complex area. This outlet mall has several shops with deeply discounted merchandise along with a food court. It can get a bit crowded during peak season there but since you are walking there, it is a nice break from crowds in the theme parks.

Chapter 6
Here Comes the Work Fun!

Day 1

Rise and shine! After a (hopefully) good night's sleep, you got up early. You've had your morning coffee and maybe a bite to eat. You've jumped into the shower and have slipped into your professional outfit. You've checked the bus schedule from your apartment to see how long it will take you to get to the Disney University. Your schedule that you received that you have to be there by 9:00 am. Since it is very important that you arrive to your first class on time, you leave a couple of hours early since you are feeling anxious and excited to be a part of the magic.

Even if this doesn't sound like you, you should consider doing this anyway. Buses have to travel on public roads to get you to your destination. Public roads carry cars driven by tourists, locals, other busses, shuttles and Cast Members driving to and from work. Anything can happen. College Program buses can break down, run late due to traffic or even get stuck in gridlock when accidents occur. Give yourself enough extra time to be able to clock in for your very first class and your scheduled shifts. No need to rack up attendance points right at the start of your program.

Having given yourself extra time, you arrive at Disney University! Your first class is usually Traditions. This class covers an overview of the History of the Walt Disney Company and Walt Disney World. The class used to take a couple of days but has been revised over the years to a class that is completed in less than eight hours. This class will be where you most likely receive your Walt Disney World Cast Nametag and Cast ID Card. Not only is it a very informative class but it is also packed with interesting fun facts about Walt and his company. Keep an eye out for opportunities to interact and volunteer in the class. Those that choose to participate might receive a prize such as a Disney Trading Pin (as an example).

Don't forget which classroom you are in. Not able to find it on your training sheet? Then how are you to find out where your class is located in the building? To figure this out, check the digital board in the lobby. It is located right as you walk in on your right hand side. When classes are in session in the early part of the day, there is usually someone at the information desk. They will be happy to direct you to your classroom location. In this lobby is also where you will clock in for your first time. As of this publication, it is a wall clock device that you will use with your Cast ID once you get it. Depending on the line of business and location you are assigned to, you will probably be using a Cast Deployment System (or CDS) to clock in and out for your day along with recording your breaks. But for now, head to your designated classroom unless the Cast Member at the information desk gives you alternate instructions.

Before your class even begins, union representatives will be there to explain their benefits of joining the union. Be sure to let the representatives know that you are a College Program Cast Member. CPs are not eligible to join the union. The representatives will most likely already know who is College Program and who isn't but just in case they give you a sign up card, just let them know you are in the program as you hand the card back to them.

There will be scheduled breaks through out your class. Do you have an issue that requires you to have to use the restroom often? Don't worry! Just chat with your facilitator ahead of time so they don't become concerned with how often nature calls for you. You don't have to worry about packing a lunch if you do not want. Fortunately, a Cast cafeteria is available to you with a hot grill and salad offerings. These do cost money and are moderately priced. Vending machines are also in the break room if you just need a snack or need to buy a beverage. Be sure to get back to your class on time. Your facilitators are on a tight schedule and will not have a lot of extra time to wait for stragglers before carrying on with your presentation.

At the end of the class, you could be given a new schedule (again depending on the line of business you are statussed to). Listen carefully to any directions that your Traditions facilitator gives you. If no other guidance is issued, congratulations on completing day one! Make sure you clock out properly. You do want to get paid correctly don't you? You can head back to your apartment and change out of the professional gear. Or maybe you have plans to meet a CP friend or new roommates at one of the parks. In any case, go relax and have fun! You have earned it!

PLEASE NOTE: It is in your best interest to get to all of your required classes on time. If you are late or miss any of these early dates, you could set your whole schedule back and have already started your program off on the wrong foot. Be responsible! Show up ready and on time! Early bird catches the worm! Well you get the picture. If you happen to blow off a class or show up late and are denied admittance into the class, your area leaders will find out. The training team spends precious time and resources setting up thousands of College Program Cast with schedules. They also schedule their trainers to be available to be with you for a specified period of days and time. When you miss your obligations, schedules have to be rearranged. Some classes are only offered on that day. To miss it could be a delay in the remainder of your training. Just understand that decisions you make early have a snowball effect.

Day 2

Good morning sunshine! Hopefully you are well rested. But realistically you are probably a bit tired. You stayed in the park late to watch the fireworks at Magic Kingdom or Epcot. I know. Believe me I understand. If it is your first time ever in the parks, the magic of Disney is magnified right now tenfold for you. There is truly no other experience like it in the world except for maybe other Disney theme parks outside of Florida. You will want to consider some kind of a routine at some point once you start seeing your weekly schedule. Getting proper rest is a key component in overall personal safety and well being. But for now, this is a good time to brew some coffee and check out your printed schedule again for today. Most lines of business have a second day of classes. Merchandise has the class Merchantainment. This class shows you how merchandise has a vital role in the overall show. You learn how to use the Point of Sale (POS) system, how to ship product to Guests resorts, homes and package pickup. You spend time learning to count change back the Disney way. Yes there is a preferred method of counting back change. The class is extremely engaging and fun!

Food and Beverage have classes around food safety. In order to work with food, you will have to take a state certification class followed immediately by a state certification test. These are very important due to the fact that Guests potentially have food allergies and food must be served properly to prevent food borne illnesses. Also you will learn about FIFO (First In First Out) to keep a close eye on expiration date and times. Don't freak out though! All states have some kind of food handler's class and testing of some kind. The state of Florida is no different. Also, when working with food, there are restrictions on what types of jewelry if any you can where while handling food. The class will cover this in full detail. Please understand that these jewelry restrictions are a state requirement and not the company being mean to you.

Operations, Entertainment and Transportation may have additional classes at Disney University but expect to have extra on the job training. Some of the roles require extensive training and almost all of the roles in these lines of business will require you to pass a check out exam. Why the check out exams? Upon successful completion of the check outs, you are able to guide Guests safely through a parking lot they are driving in; you are able to safely operate and evacuate an attraction; you are able to safely handle Guest flow when working with a character team. All of these are important and revolve around safety. Safety for the Guests and Cast Members like yourself is extremely important and vital to protecting the magic along with show integrity.

Once you have completed your second day, check to see if your on-boarding schedule (area training) has been altered. If your sheet is not clear in its instructions speak to your facilitator right away. They can look into it for you before you leave your training class. Very rarely does this occur unless you missed one of your early training days. Head back to your apartment or go unwind and enjoy the magic but make sure you follow your schedule closely. You are most likely heading to your work location for your scheduled day three.

Area Training

All right! You are up bright and early again. You might even be saying to yourself, "Wow! I can handle these daytime shifts. No Problem!" Now hold on there a second. Remember, this is just a training schedule. You will be seeing your real schedule start and end times soon. Get yourself ready to start your day. If you haven't already ventured out to get your costumes (some classes require you to do just that), then head in to your location extra early to go check out those costumes. When you arrive, there are very helpful Costuming Cast Members that can tell you which aisles you will need to go to get each of your costuming pieces. If any of the required pieces are not available, you should receive a slip of paper to give to your area. This paper explains that there is a costuming exemption. This means that although you may not be in exact Disney Look, you are given a temporary exemption from scrutiny. Just check back the next day to see if the correct piece is back in.

There is a chance that your first day will be either a whole day of touring your location or a half day tour and half day with a trainer. The parks, resorts and Downtown Disney (soon to be Disney Springs) have a multi hour tour for new Cast Members that require you to dress in professional dress and wear good walking shoes. These tours are not only informative but extremely fun. The purpose is to give you perspective and allow you to become accustomed to your new surroundings. Whether it comes before your area training or after, just know that it is on your training plan. This is another class that you do not want to be late for. Consider yourself warned.

Costuming sizes are not true sizing! If you wear a size 30 waist in pants, you may be looking at a larger costuming size. And even if you find your size there, one pair of that size might fit and a similar one will not. Nobody really knows why this phenomenon exists. It just does. Try on all of your pieces and find the right costume that fits your body type correctly. You have on the right costume. You've checked yourself out dozens of times in the full length mirrors. Don't feel bad if you feel like you don't look good in your costume. The costumes are designed to meet a specific theme or need and they are not necessarily there to create a fashion statement. Everyone experiences this phenomenon at some point. Just know you are not alone in this issue. Also, make sure you have purchased the correct type of shoes! Your initial costuming sheet will tell you specifically what type of shoes you should have. Avoid anything flashy with large logos. Most shoe types required are all black or all white. Whether they are shoes that need to be polished or tennis shoes, this will be stated in your costuming sheet. Don't have a lot of money to spend on shoes? Fortunately, places like Wal-Mart sell inexpensive shoes that will at least last you until your first official paycheck. Don't forget a comfortable shoe insert! Take care of your feet. You will most likely be spending a lot of your day walking around. Now it is time to meet your trainer.

Be sure to follow the instructions for that day. If your schedule says meet your trainer in costuming, then meet them on time at costuming. Your trainer will wait in the designated location for a finite period of time. If you do not show within say ten to fifteen minutes, they will probably be calling their office to find out what your status is. Your smiling trainer should be there on time and ready to greet you. If you happen to be waiting more than ten minutes, you should be able to use a house phone at you designated meeting spot. You can call Deployment or the Training Office. Just make sure you note the time and pay attention to any changes in instructions.

The goal is to still make sure that you are credited for being to work on time with no attendance issues.

In a perfect world, your trainer is on time and you are on time. Do take note that I said "a perfect world". Sometimes things happen and a trainer could be sick. Don't panic. Just call the phone number on your training sheet or Cast Deployment. Someone else will be assigned to you at that point. They will then show you where you will be clocking in at your work location. Be prepared for a long day today though. Your first day in the area is typically an overview day. So what happens on an overview day you ask? Plan on a lot of walking and most likely sitting in front of a computer doing required e-learning classes. Your trainer will be bringing you to your specific work location. You will be introduced to some of your leaders (whoever is working at that moment), some of the Cast members that are working and possibly your Area Manager if all goes well on the timing. What typically occurs is that your trainer is on time but you didn't pre-scout your area to know where you need to be. You are frantically trying to figure out where you should be and are now about ten minutes late to clock in for you shift. It isn't the end of the world but it does feel like you have gotten off on the wrong foot with your trainer and your area. You really should consider going by your work area before your official day so you can determine where you are supposed to meet your trainer.

If you are in resorts as a Concierge Host or Hostess, you will get to see where your work stations are, the break rooms, the Cast bathrooms and any area that you will need to be familiar with. You will learn about important locations within your resort that are important to the Guests and the Guest experience. You will also be learning about all kinds of cool things you can do including but not limited to: checking in Guests to your resort, assisting Guests with their passes to attractions and even dining reservations / cancelations. Think of your role in Concierge as a resort version of Guest Relations. It's not exactly like it but it is definitely close according to former College Program Cast that I have spoken to.

Operations and Merchandise in the parks will be walking their designated lands to gain overall knowledge of what is available to Guests in addition to seeing where they will be training hands on. No matter what line of business you are in, just be mindful that this first day in the area is long. The e-learning and tour are required in order to help set you up for long term success. As you wrap up your first day in your area, take comfort in knowing that your next shift should be hands on and working directly with Guests. Some areas might alter this portion on how they facilitate it but for the most part, training prefers to keep the process the same from park to park. This way it makes it familiar and easier for those College Program Cast that change their location during their program or if they happen to do a second program in a different location.

On the Job Training

Another day is upon you and it's time to head into work! Be sure to get to your designated clock in location on time. You are probably not meeting your trainer in the original place you met them yesterday. Your trainer should have established this with you during your previous training day. So clock in and get ready! You will most likely be working with Guests today.

So what does working with Guests look like for you? Merchandise will have you on register training. Even though your first several transactions might be in training mode and not working with Guests, there will be a point (if your trainer feels confident in your learning abilities) that you will be live. They will be checking to see if you remember how to offer and facilitate package delivery, talking to Guests about their day or offering information that Guests will find invaluable and thanking them after the end. Now there are other things they will look for as well such as counting back the Disney way but the previous aforementioned are vital to the overall Guest experience.

In Operations and Entertainment, you will be learning the ropes and the focus will be safety, safety, safety! Attractions College

Program Cast will specifically be learning all of the important rules, regulations and proper procedures on how to operate, spiel and evacuate locations properly. You must learn all of these functions inside and out. It is your responsibility to preserve show quality, integrity and Cast / Guest safety.

Custodial Cast learns about the nuances involved with keeping the magic clean and assisting all lines of operations in the advent that a Guest or Cast Member become ill. There are many locations throughout the property that contain many bathrooms, cleaning supplies and safety equipment. You will want to learn where your area specific locations are for these locations.

For those in Transportation, I didn't forget about you folks! Your role is just as important as any role there! You set the tone for Guests' day. You will be learning and checking out on your knowledge of proper loading procedures in parking, Monorail safety, Tram Driving safety, Tram spiels and assisting Guests with locating their vehicles. Of course what you learn specifically will depend on what you have signed up for. But just know that safety is a number one priority and focus of your role at all times.

Extended Learning

Once your initial couple of days of required training is complete, you could be looking at additional classes and e-learning down the road. Don't forget: Food and Beverage Cast must take the state food handling certification. Does your role in Transportation require you to have a CDL? As a College Program Cast Member, probably not but be sure to prepare for the test if you do. Are you working in Glow sales? You are probably looking at a separate day for Glow and Apron Cash Handling training. Training is unavoidable regardless of where you work. Once you get through it successfully, you will begin to see the real program emerge!

Time to Go Work!

Take a deep breath. The initial training has concluded. You have been given so much information over the last few days. Don't allow yourself to feel overwhelmed. Everyone started off in your position at one point or another. When I say everyone I do mean EVERYONE. Everyone who has ever worked at Walt Disney World (including myself) had to go through training and spend a few weeks post training with the "Earning My Ears" tag on our nametags. Guests understand that those tags mean you are a newbie, a green horn, a rookie...brand new. Guests will most likely strike up a conversation with you once they realize you are new to the company.

"How do you like working here?" "Where are you from?" "Oh, a student? What is your major?" These are common questions you will get but know these are also excellent ice breaker questions to help ease you into the Guest Service part of your role. One of the statements I enjoy sharing with Guests over the years when they asked if I liked working there was: "It's fantastic! I get paid to talk to people like yourself." Now that is a shortened generalization of what I do daily but there is some truth to this concept. At the time, I was a leader in Merchandise. In typical merchandise locations outside of Disney, there is a requirement to pressure sell products. Sure this is talking to people but it is more of a method of getting people to buy items whether they need them or not. Have you ever been to a mall department store? Who doesn't absolutely love a cologne or perfume sales clerk stepping in your walking path and spraying you with some fragrance or another then trying to convince you to step up to the counter. Or how about the never annoying mall kiosks where a sales clerk or two are trying to literally pull you over to force a sale. Ah these experiences are so much fun. Aren't they? By the way, I was being completely sarcastic. Some people like this approach but then there is me. I can't stand it one bit.

What exactly do I mean by being paid to talk to people then? Glad you asked! Think about where you are signed up to work. It doesn't matter which line of business for your College Program. Your role will most likely be associated with heavy Guest contact. You will have specific requirements of your job but understand that the company encourages being engaging with the Guests. Letting Guests know about items available for sale in shops are great but you do not work in a mall. Talking to Guests about park and resort offerings are common conversations. Guests like to ask for advice on where to go and what to eat. Have fun with your Guests! Create magical moments! Use the tools that your work area supplies you with to create those special one on one moments. Guest satisfaction is a high priority and how you choose to engage with your Guests also is reflected in their overall satisfaction.

Area Support

So your training is over. You now are coming in to work on time for your shift and following your work assignment. I guess your all on your own now. There won't be anybody around to assist you when you need it. You are in effect a complete expert in your work location. Don't worry. Nobody is expecting you to be a complete expert in everything. Each area has leaders, coordinators and peers. These people are invaluable resources that you will probably be leaning heavily on during the early stages of your College Program. Don't feel bad about relying on them. They are probably expecting it. Practice makes perfect. Also, they are there to make sure that you don't take shortcuts. Shortcuts can mean the difference between a safe and unsafe environment. Never take shortcuts on safety. Make sure that if you have a checklist of chores or safety procedures that you follow through and complete them all within the time allotted. The point to all of this is that if you have questions or are unsure, consult your resources. Get clarification. It is always better to ask for clarification and proceed correctly than to guess or attempt to figure out the answer on your own. Utilize your resources wisely.

Everyday will bring new challenges. Consider each day as a new learning experience because it will be. Keep in mind that no two days are exactly alike especially when you have Guests arriving and departing daily. New people bring new experiences!

Breaks

Everyone needs a break from work from time to time. Breaks are an important part of your working day. Skipping breaks are not an option. There should be posted guidelines in your location that explain what the federal or state guidelines are on breaks. Breaks are required and should be taken within the time you are scheduled for. Here comes something important for you to know: **make sure that you take your full break and return to your work area on time!** Do not try and sneak extra time or take extra breaks. Your peers also have break times and their ability to take that break on time is contingent on your promptly going to break on time and returning on time as well. Be sure to check with your trainer, leaders or coordinators about how your break is facilitated. Each work area has somewhat different procedures for facilitating breaks. As an example, parks Cast Members pick up their breaks differently from resort Cast Members.

What's the big deal? Nobody is paying attention to when I sign in or out for breaks. Five extra minutes won't hurt anyone. WRONG! People create your breaks. They create all Cast breaks. Whether it's on CDS or on break sheets, the times are based on when you start your day, the demands of the business area and the break needs of others. If you decide to take an extra minute or two or five or more means that someone else is falling behind from taking their break and (quite frankly) you are stealing company time. Yes...I did say steal as in theft. These antics can cause you grief and possible disciplinary action if you continuously abuse break privileges. There could be times where your area is so busy that it cannot afford to let you go to break on time or you could get caught with a Guest service situation. Be sure to communicate with your coordinators and or leaders. You will still get your break.

Have you been standing outside working for what seems like an eternity? You are still waiting on your break to show up in CDS? Ask yourself "what time did I start my day?" As a rule of thumb, if four hours have gone by and your break hasn't shown up, I would call my Coordinator first and if none are available I would call my Manager on Duty (MOD). Longer than four hours means that there might be a bigger issue that needs to be addressed. Maybe a Cast Member called out and none of the breaks are going out on time. Rest assured that Cast Deployment are probably already in contact with your coordinators and leaders making them aware of the issue. But it never hurts to check for yourself. Just because your break hasn't shown up after two hours doesn't mean that there is an issue. So again, don't panic.

Just to recap here because it is very important: make sure you take your breaks on time and return on time. Even if you see others taking longer, do not fall into their trap. You can only control your own actions. People abusing breaks will have to suffer their own consequences. Consider yourself warned on this topic as well!

Pay Attention to Your Surroundings

This is a phrase you may hear a lot especially in your training days but it can also be a very vague statement. What this statement means to me can be broken up into a few parts. Those parts are: know what is around you to enhance the Guest Experience, know your area's emergency plan and know where to find the resources you need to be successful each day. So let's break each of these down to their core meanings.

To know what is around you to enhance the Guest Experience means that you need to be able to answer some basic questions that Guests will have before answering the more complex ones. What is a basic question? "Where is the closest restroom, bathroom or water closet"? All three are asking the same question but are asked differently based on where you are from geographically on the globe. You should know where the closest restroom is from any point where you are working. Parks have many restrooms spread out so knowing your park map intimately will be beneficial for you. It would be sad if you sent a Guest to use the restrooms up in the front of the park when there is one located just outside your store or attraction or even in your restaurant. A Guests time is precious to them. They will be waiting in lines even though they have a few passes to get on attractions quickly. Every minute you can save them is valuable to their experience.

"Where is the closest smoking section?" If you don't know this answer immediately, grab a map or ask a peer. These locations change locations from time to time based on resort or park needs. But taking the time to know where they are located could help save non-smoking Guests unnecessary aggravation with those that smoke.

"Where is the exit, monorail or the way to the parking lot?" You really should know how to exit your park or resort from any point that you are standing. The buildings and locations are so impressive that Guests can become confused. Just because they aren't familiar with your location doesn't mean that you can't become a hero for them at that moment.

The questions above are what I consider the top three questions you will get on any given day. There will be others that pop up often like: "What time is the parade? Where is a good place to view it? Where is the closest place to eat or get ice cream or get funnel cakes? Where can I get a turkey leg? Do you have a pin trading lanyard on? Where is the Harry Potter area?" And yes, people actually believe that Disney owns everything and some might even swear to you that they remember seeing it in one of the Disney parks! I know it sounds crazy but this happens. The other answers to these questions will take time and probably assistance from your peers to answer. But hang in there! You are almost an expert in your area now and you have only been here a few weeks!

If you are in Florida, understand that at certain times of the year discussions around tropical storms and hurricanes take place. The state has a storied history of severe storms. With this history comes learning and planning. The Walt Disney World Resort has a safety group that plans out their emergency contingency for such events. Your individual area will also have a safety plan as well. It is important that you never panic when such an event looks to be anywhere near the area. Always follow the instructions of your coordinators and leaders. These instructions are designed to keep everyone safe and safety will always be the highest priority. You will also want to consider having a hurricane or tropical storm survival kit for your apartment. Items like: bottled water, emergency radio, batteries, flashlight, non-perishable food and a first aid kit are always good to have even when there isn't a storm warning. Most of these items can be found at places like Wal-Mart and Target.

To be set up for success each day, know where a Guest can purchase or acquire basic first aid supplies, sundries, water fountains (everyone needs to stay hydrated) and where the closest location to find a wheelchair for a Guest. Sometimes Guests become dehydrated and just need a place to sit down in the shade. If a bench isn't available, attractions sometimes carry transport wheelchairs that can be used temporarily for Guest needs.

Conflict

When temperatures rise or people from different backgrounds and beliefs come together in a close work environment, tempers can become flared. While at work, do not allow yourself to become engaged in any arguments or aggressive discussions with Guests or other Cast. These dramatic conversations never work out well for the Cast. Under no circumstances should any type of flagrant or derogatory foul language words or phrases should ever be uttered on stage or backstage. If the right person hears you swearing and reports it, you may have just caused your program to end abruptly. If you swear at or get into a physical confrontation with a Guest, you will most likely be going moving out of College Program Housing, seeing possibly legal ramifications if violence was involved and having to go home and explain to family or friends what happened. This embarrassing situation is easily avoidable. If you are being approached by an aggressive Guest, continue to smile regardless of their statements and contact your MOD (Manager on Duty). They are paid to take the brunt of a Guest's anger and should be there to help shield you from their angst. Just do not do anything to inflame the issue. If you are having an issue with a peer, you will want to contact your MOD. Again, do not add fuel to an emotional fire.

Conflict typically doesn't happen often. You can go days or even weeks with no major conflict. But just remember to stay calm and follow proper protocol when conflict situations do arise. Temperatures might not be the only reason why conflict starts. People who haven't had any food in their body or even just their experiences leading up to that particular moment could have caused their attitude to boil over. It is important to never take conflict personally and to move on to your excellent Guest Service skills once it has been resolved.

Recognition

Recognition is very important to the Cast experience. I mean who doesn't like to be recognized for a job well done? I not only loved working with Cast Recognition, I loved planning and executing recognition events. When planned properly, they are a fantastic way to engage directly with my Cast and peers. Maybe I also just thoroughly enjoyed seeing the smiles on my Cast faces when our event or party was a success! Every area has some kind of Cast Recognition. It could come in the form of a pot luck party where everyone has a chance to sign up and bring in a food dish. It could also come in an area specific or resort / park specific catered party. Whatever the event, you should try and attend and get in on the fun! When these big events take place, you will be able to enjoy free food, dance, character meet and greets, door prizes, trivia and much more! I always loved giving out movie tickets and DVDs to Cast as a part of my area's recognition program. And my area liked to partner with an adjoining area to do one big end of year Cast party for our areas. We would pick a theme like Frozen or Big Hero 6 and then play trivia games and have raffle prizes while also having the event catered for the Cast. So much food and fun prizes awaited our Cast each year!

The great thing about these recognition events as well is that you are able to attend them in costume when you are working. You will still need to follow regular work procedures and attend the event on your break(s) but they also tend to go for extended hours. This helps the various shifts to be able to attend. If you aren't sure about the event requirements, ask one of your leaders for clarification. Remember: there is still a business to be run. Even though the recognition event is about you, there are still Guests to be serviced and breaks to be given to your peers.

Chapter 7
Time for Fun!

Well you have been given a lot of information overall during your first several days. You have spent quality time at Disney University learning in your required classes including Traditions. You have been given your first real schedule (non-training). Even though the information may seem overwhelming at first, you begin to see that it looks to be pretty straight forward. Training may or may not have been tiring or even downright exhausting. You've been practicing your Disney Point (two fingers or whole hand) when talking to strangers. You may even start feeling compelled to pick up trash while using correct safety methods that you have just earned while walking through your apartment complex. Don't worry; these are skills that you will be taking with you for the remainder of your days. But that's alright. You are quickly growing as a person! Time to take a breather and play!

Play in The Parks!

The company encourages its Cast Members to play in the parks. It helps you get familiar with the attractions and offerings. This knowledge is considerably helpful when you are working and talking with Guests. Maybe you experienced a show or a place to eat? This could be very helpful to a Guest's overall experience. Don't be afraid to share your knowledge. Guests love to come back and share the news of how you helped make their trip that much more magical. This is one of the many perks you get as a Disney Cast Member. Keep in mind that if family is in town joining you, you will want to be mindful of how many times you are able to use your Maingate pass. Cast Members can go into the parks as much as they want (minus block out dates) but your Maingate pass (to get friends and family into the parks) is limited.

UPDATE: As of press time, CPs accrue Maingate tickets based on the amount of hours worked! Check with your leadership team for how this process works.

Each of the parks has different different offerings and experiences. They also all have different park hours. Make sure you check out the actual park times before you travel there. The My Disney Experience application is a great resource on your smartphone. You can also look this information up on the disneyworld.com website as well. Fireworks times also tend to vary throughout the year as well. Don't worry about cramming every park experience into your first couple of days. You have time to enjoy it over the duration of your program!

Something else for you to consider though is signing up for your own account on the My Disney Experience app. You have the ability to link your Maingate pass to your account along with your Guest passes. This comes in handy if you plan on going to a specific park each time you play and want to try and sign up for a Fastpass for a couple of attractions. Just be aware that you might not be able to sign up for exact attractions you want because availability is based on what is still available. Guests and Cast are utilizing this same process and some attraction Fastpasses are claimed faster than others. Now you do not have to try for Fastpasses on the app only. You can come into a park day of and try to sign up at one of the kiosks in the park. Just keep in mind that they are distributed on a first come first served basis.

Did you happen to wander into a park or resort shop and see a fun MagicBand that caught your eye? These fun accessories can be purchased and linked to your My Disney Experience app. If you and your family are staying in a resort when they visit you, you will be issued on automatically. It is your room key to enter your room. It can be your admission into the park if you like a park ticket to your band whether it is a complimentary band from your resort or purchased in a Disney shop. You can also decorate your band with any of the fun MagicBand accessories that are available throughout various shops on Disney property.

Rather Do Something Else?

Your College Program Transportation buses have routes to The Florida Mall & grocery stores. Look for the occasional announcements for bus trips to Tampa for football or baseball excursions through the Cast publication: Eyes & Ears.

Thinking about going to Sea World to feed the sea lions or check out the penguin exhibit? Maybe you were looking to go to Universal Studios Orlando and check out the multi-park Harry Potter experiences? You will need to have a car with you, make friends with a Cast Member who has a car or seek alternate transportation. These are further away and your CP transportation buses do not travel to these locations. There are also several outlet malls with discounted products in the area. But again, it will take transportation to get you to these shopping gems.

Or maybe you are just looking to get away from the craziness of crowds, traffic and work. Want to go to the beaches in Florida? Florida has some of the most picturesque beaches in the country! And Florida is surrounded by beaches and blue water on three sides! Uber and Lyft could take you there but it could add up. From Disney, Cocoa Beach (Atlantic Coast) is approximately a 45 minute to an hour drive and Clearwater (Gulf Coast) is about an hour drive depending on traffic and time of day.

What else is there available to do? What are you interested in or what have you wanted to try? Central Florida is quite unique in its offerings. Here is a list of some of the Central Florida attractions and their addresses:

Universal Studios Orlando - 6000 Universal Blvd, Orlando, FL 32819

Sea World - 7007 Sea World Dr, Orlando, FL 32821

Legoland - 1 Legoland Way, Winter Haven, FL 33884

Busch Gardens Tampa - 10165 N Malcolm McKinley Dr, Tampa, FL 33612

Seminole Hard Rock Hotel and Casino Tampa - 5223 N Orient Road, Tampa, FL 33610

Daytona International Speedway - 1801 W International Speedway Blvd, Daytona Beach, FL 32114

Bok Tower Gardens - 1151 Tower Blvd, Lake Wales, FL 33853

The Orlando Eye - 8401 International Drive #100, Orlando, FL 32819

Pointe Orlando - 9101 International Dr #1600, Orlando, FL 32819

Orlando International Premium Outlet Mall - 4951 International Drive, Orlando, FL 32819

Lake Buena Vista Factory Stores - 15657 Kissimmee Vineland Rd, Orlando, FL 32821

Gatorland - 14501 S Orange Blossom Trl, Orlando, FL 32837

AMC Theaters - Downtown Disney (soon to be Disney Springs) and Universal City Walk

House of Blues Restaurant - Downtown Disney (soon to be Disney Springs)

Planet Hollywood Restaurant - Downtown Disney (soon to be Disney Springs)

Regal Cinemas - (at Pointe Orlando)

Cinepolis Polk County IMAX - 5500, Grandview Pkwy, Davenport, FL 33837

Bubba Gump Restaurant - Universal City Walk

Jimmy Buffet's Margaritaville - Universal City Walk

Cowfish Orlando Restaurant - Universal City Walk

Helicopter Tours on I-Drive - 8990 International Dr, Orlando, FL 32819

Ice Bar Orlando - 8967 International Dr, Orlando, FL 32819

Gators Dockside - 601 Cagan Park Ave. Bldg #4, Clermont, FL 34714

Miller's Orlando Ale House - 12371 Winter Garden Vineland Road, Orlando, FL 32836

Want to watch the big game at a sports bar? The Miller's Orlando Ale House (mentioned above) and any of the many Buffalo Wild Wings Restaurants are fantastic places to throw on your favorite sports jersey, order up some hot wings and cheer on your favorite teams!

Sporting Events Are Quite Popular Here!

Do you like sports? Florida has two MLB teams (Miami Marlins and Tampa Bay Rays), three NFL teams (Miami Dolphins, Jacksonville Jaguars & Tampa Bay Buccaneers), two NBA teams (Orlando Magic & Miami Heat), two NHL teams (Florida Panthers & Tampa Bay Lightning), one MLS team (Orlando City Soccer Club). Don't forget to check the Cast store: Company D. Sometimes they offer discounted tickets to these sporting events. During the spring, the Atlanta Braves MLB Team (currently) uses the ESPN Wide World of Sports as their Citrus League stadium for spring training. There are other teams that play spring training games in the Sunshine State as well. The closest teams besides the Atlanta Braves include: the Houston Astros (Kissimmee, FL) and Detroit Tigers (Lakeland, FL).They also offer discounted movie tickets and Cast exclusive merchandise. Did you know that there are actually baseball fields on Disney Property that aren't a part of the ESPN Wide World of Sports Complex? It's true! They are located closer to the warehouses and Downtown Disney area (soon to be Disney Springs). At different times of the year, Cast Activities has Cast softball leagues that Cast can participate in. These leagues may have a nominal registration fee but they can be a lot of fun to participate in if you are so inclined.

Prefer college sports? UCF, Florida State, University of Florida and Miami receive a lot of attention in this state. Some college football bowl games are played in this state as well. Once college football and basketball seasons are in full swing, you will most likely see more people walking around the resort and parks wearing their school colors and jerseys.

But What About Inexpensive Outings?

But wait! Didn't I mention earlier that there were inexpensive things to do? After all, you did plan on budgeting your money to stay within your means...right? So besides the four Disney theme parks, everything else mentioned costs money. Isn't there anything else you can do? There is! The Disney water parks (Typhoon Lagoon and

Blizzard Beach) occasionally advertise free admissions or discounted admissions to Cast Members. These parks are a lot of fun and can be relaxing when it isn't considered peak season. Oh and who doesn't enjoy grabbing a floating tube and relaxing in the lazy river? It's a great way to grab some sunshine and take a leisurely float down the moving river. Ugh! Did somebody just squirt me with water? I didn't come to the water park to get...wet. Okay maybe I'm overreacting but I have actually heard people say those exact words. It never loses its humor when you hear it. And are you brave enough to ride what I refer to as the atomic wedgies? Summit Plummet is definitely high up but it is intensely fun! There are lockers available to rent so you can protect your valuables and electronics. Consult the Disney HUB for block out dates and specials currently running.

Marathons

Like to go for a good run or a jog for exercise? Keeping up on your personal health and enjoying the time working out can be extremely rewarding. And Walt Disney World hosts a few marathon events throughout the year that can help you keep up on your exercising and personal health. When signups for the marathons occur, they tend to sell out real fast. But if you're quick enough you can not only sign up for a marathon event but you can also save a few dollars as a Cast Member too! These marathon races are so much fun! Characters are placed along the course for photo opportunities and water stations are present too. ESPN Wide World of Sports has a race expo during race weekends which can be attended by anyone. Many vendors are on hand selling discounted race gear to help you gear up and in some cases gear up in Disney themed gear! Be sure to check out the Disney HUB for the Cast Member discount promo code for the races. To sign up for a marathon, you would need to go to the internet site: **rundisney.com**

UPDATE:

The Florida races are for 2017 (subject to change each year):
- Walt Disney World Marathon Weekend presented by Cigna - January 4th through the 8th, 2017
- Disney Princess Half Marathon Weekend presented by the Children's Miracle Network Hospitals - February 23rd through the 26th, 2017
- Star War Half Marathon: The Dark Side – April 20th through 23rd, 2017
- Virtual Running Shorts – June 1st through August 31st, 2017
- Disney Wine and Dine Half Marathon Weekend presented by MISFIT – November 2nd through 5th, 2017

Disney property isn't the only location in Central Florida that has marathons. They are actually quite common in Orlando and in locations like Celebration, Clermont, Winter Garden and Lakeland. The cost of these races is historically less expensive than the Disney races. A great resource for locating these resources is the website: **runningintheusa.com**

Ooh...Mini Golf

Disney also has two miniature golf courses (Fantasia & Winter Summerland) which are very reasonably priced for Cast Members as well. The Fantasia course is themed out featuring familiar elements from the Disney animated classic: Fantasia. Look out for those water hazards! You'll understand what I mean once you try the course. And Winter Summerland courses are interesting because they are both themed out Christmas but one side features Santa Clause during the summer and the other...you guessed it. Santa Clause during the winter. Both are comical and a lot of fun especially for groups of friends and families.

Downtown Disney (soon to be renamed Disney Springs) boasts a large movie theater, bowling alley and various other shops and lounge areas that are great for relaxing and atmosphere. Most locations here offer a Disney Cast Member discount. And they have just recently added car boat rentals which are incredibly cool to watch and a lot of fun to ride in!

During the later part of the year, Cast have an opportunity to try out for the Epcot Candlelight Processional. This incredible event is performed by Cast Members (singing) while an invited special celebrity Guest tells the story of the first Christmas. Celebrity Guest Speakers vary from date to date and year to year. Your participation (if picked) in rehearsals determines how many dates you are able to participate in. Even if you choose not to participate, it is incredible to watch as a Guest and I highly recommend it to Cast to see at least once.

Okay are you looking for mini golf that isn't on Disney property? There are several around town! Some are pirate themed and some are jungle themed. If you happen to be driving anywhere Crossroads on Hwy 535 near CP housing, there is a mini golf place near there. Also by Target on Hwy 192 there is one there as well. Both are within a fifteen minute drive of your apartment housing.

Holiday Ticketed Events

Also during the Halloween season and Christmas season are ticketed events (also known as hard ticket events). Mickey's Not So Scary Halloween Party takes place from early September through the end of October on select nights. Company D (the Cast store) will offer Cast discounted tickets on select nights. The event allows Guests with tickets to go to predetermined areas to "Trick or Treat" while showing off their costumes (if wearing any) and several special surprises only available at the event. The parade for this event is incredible! Exclusive merchandise is also available during the party nights only. The other major holiday event is Mickey's Very Merry Christmas Party. This event takes place from November until a week or so before Christmas. Instead of Trick or Treat locations, they have hot cocoa and sugar cookie stations. Exclusive Merchandise and a special parade are also available on those select nights. PLEASE

NOTE: If you can't do sugar, there is usually a sugar free option at both parties.

Oh! Maybe you were thinking about wandering over to Magic Kingdom to be a part of the Christmas Day parade? You've seen it on television so it should be fun...right? WRONG! First, Cast are blocked out during the weeks of Christmas and New Years. Second, the parade is actually filmed weeks prior Christmas. Sorry to ruin the magic for you but the broadcasts do say at various times previously filmed, taped earlier or something to that effect depending on the station that televises it for you. If you pay close attention to communications released to the Cast, you might possibly learn about opportunities to be involved in the taping. The key is to pay close attention. The spots fill up quick and you must meet the requirements that are listed. You won't be able to miss out on work for the taping. It is done on your own personal time. Sad I know. But hey it is another possible perk of the job!

Speaking of Disney Cast Member discount, many shops and restaurants and services offered off property off a Disney Cast Member discount. Don't be afraid to ask. The worse that will happen is that somebody says no. Your Cast Services location (near your work space) or the Cast store: Company D usually carries a copy of the Cast Incredible Discounts booklet. This booklet is extremely informative and can help you in locating which companies are offering discounts. Discounts include but are not limited to: Automotive, Travel, Dining, Entertainment, Pet care, Apartments, House Buying & Banking.

Mickey's Retreat

None of these interest you? You do have an option that is only available to Disney Cast and up to the amount of allotments that are issued to you on your Maingate. Mickey's Retreat is a Cast only hideaway that offers Cast relaxation and recreation. It is located near Chatham Square Apartments at: 8151 Lake Forest Dr, Orlando, FL

32821. They are open from morning until dusk and are staffed by Cast Members. It does not cost anything for Cast Members or their dependants to enter but some services might have a fee while there. The Cast HUB should have up to date information on events and offerings available to you. The location has a swimming pool, volleyball locations along with lounge chairs to lie out and grab some sunshine.

Other things to do: skydiving lessons, helicopter tours, airboat tours, fishing excursions, marathons and pub crawls (for those over 21) to name a few. A few years ago, I was fortunate to sign up to become a scuba certified diver through NAUI. It is advertised occasionally through Cast communications. If you were ever thinking about doing this, I highly recommend this! The cost to get certified is much cheaper than if you went for certification through an outside trainer. All of my lessons were at Mickey's Retreat on select days. The check out dive was in a fresh water lake in Central Florida. It is a fantastic experience and once certified, you can sign up for one of the scuba diving excursions at Epcot (if they are still offered at the time you are certified). One of my most cherished memories was diving the aquarium tank at Epcot. Can you imagine? You are diving in the large tank while Guests dine in the Coral Reef Restaurant. I've done it! People waving and taking pictures of you as you pass by the window as they eat. It is a surreal experience to say the least. Words cannot truly describe the awesomeness of this one of a kind experience.

Whatever you decide to do for fun and recreation, plan ahead! Tickets to events go quickly for Cast events. They are typically sold on a first come first served basis. For excursions not Disney related, look online for discount coupons, codes or promos. There are many times that places like Universal or Sea World offer discount codes online. The Orlando Eye offers the best rate for their attractions online. If you buy them in person, you will be paying a lot more than you should. But you don't have a laptop or computer available you say? Hopefully by now you have a smartphone. I know there are some people who are holdouts and do not want to bothered by technology. If that description fits you, check to see if you have a resource center available in your workplace or at your apartment complex. You can print out your discount coupons or ticket purchases at these locations. Saving even a few dollars is better than no dollars. Right?

How to Play In the Parks While On a Budget

Even though you are paid for your internship, you aren't making so much money that you could play in the parks like a regular day Guest. If you happen to have money already saved to be able to do just that then congratulations! But assuming if you are like most College Program Cast Members, you will need to have a solid plan for budgeting your way through a day at the theme parks. While I continuously run the risk of sounding obvious even here, start off by planning to eat some of your meals at home whether it is before you go or after. Paying in park prices for food especially when you are there almost all day can add up fast! You can also consider packing some snacks with you. Do you have a drawstring backpack? This would definitely come in handy and well worth the trip through the bag check line. It is so much easier on the pocket book when you only really have to worry about purchasing a beverage or just using the many water fountains on property. If you really feel the need to immerse yourself in the overall experience, just pick one meal to purchase so this way you aren't committing to buying three meals. Breakfast offerings are limited and the ones out there might only be reservation only at sit down restaurants. Lunch or dinner is easier to do with the many quick service offerings out there. Want to save some money on buying a beverage? Head over to a merchandise location that sells bottled beverages. At that location you get your regular Cast Discount on the drink. If you plan accordingly for an all day adventure in the parks, you could make it through the day by spending about $20 for your day. I derived this total from factoring in that you did eat at least breakfast at home; purchased a bottle of water and refilled it throughout the day at the park water fountains; had a simple snack at one of the healthy choice stands; purchased a moderate late lunch or early dinner; and maybe enjoyed an ice cream bar or a scoop of ice cream. Need a souvenir from your play day? Park maps are complimentary and celebration buttons are complimentary at various shops and Guest Relations.

Is Living On A Budget Possible During Your Program?

But what about your program? Budgeting for a park day is nice but you have an entire program to think about. Is it possible to go through your whole program and spend very little money and survive? Of course it is possible! People live within their means all the time! A former Cast Member of mine shared for me a unique strategy that he and his brother used when they were a part of the College Program. He had saved all of his pay minus the few expenses of food he purchased. He didn't wander far from work, the parks or home and had a nice nest egg to take home. Now the quality of food may not have been the best and I believed he spoke of eating ramen a lot but it can be done. Is that completely practical to do? Not really. He is a special breed of person that likes to sock his hard earned money away for a rainy day and enjoy only the free things available to him. I even remember telling him that he could have at least splurged a little bit since fruits and vegetables aren't that expensive. You can eat well balanced and not go broke doing so. And you do not need to eat ramen every day and only play in the parks; you can still enjoy your time in and around Orlando without having to go broke. Just remember to follow your budget plan.

Ever Dreamed of Taking a Cruise?

Since you are in Florida, you may not have known that this state has three major cruise ports. There is Port Canaveral, Tampa and Miami that are homes to major cruise lines. The heart of your program may not be conducive for you to break away for a cruise excursion but many CPs look at taking a cruise and sometimes even their very first cruise right after their program concludes. Think of it as a way of celebrating a successful conclusion to your college program with Disney. Before you leave the program, you can always check the Disney HUB for any Cast discounted cruises through the Disney Cruise Line. With Port Canaveral within an hour's drive, you could find a short excursion that fits your needs. If taking a cruise is important to you, I have included some information for some of the companies that launch from Florida ports.

Port Canaveral Cruise Lines:
- Carnival - 9245 Charles M Rowland Dr, Port Canaveral, FL 32920
  You can book online at carnival.com
- Disney Cruise Line - 9155 Charles M Rowland Dr, Port Canaveral, FL 32920
  You can book online at disneycruise.com
- Royal Caribbean - 9005 Charles M Rowland Dr, Cape Canaveral, FL 32920
  You can book online at royalcaribbean.com
- Norwegian - 9241 Charles M Rowland Dr, Cape Canaveral, FL 32920
  You can book online at ncl.com

Port of Tampa Cruise Lines:
- Carnival (carnival.com) - 651 Channelside Drive, Tampa, FL 33602
- Holland America (hollandamerica.com) - 1333 McKay Street, Tampa, FL 33602
- Royal Caribbean (royalcaribbean.com) - 815 Channelside Drive, Tampa, FL 33602

Chapter 8
Your College Program and Relationships

Relationships

Many people come to the program with absolutely no intention to get involved with anyone in a relationship. Reasons vary from already having a relationship back home or that you would rather focus all of your available energy and channeling it into your program. But sometimes relationships just form or happen. There is never any real rhyme or reason as to why or how but they just do happen occasionally. Relationships can be a beautiful thing. Sure they can have their ups and downs. Nothing in life is ever perfect and that also is true of most relationships. But they can be an awesome experience. Whether you have a relationship before you arrive or meet someone and fall in love during your program, you will still want to be smart about your personal life when working. Relationships can come in all kinds of types. Remember that Disney celebrates Diversity and that includes relationship of all recognized types. It doesn't matter if the relationship is a guy and girl, girl and girl or guy and guy. You still need to remember that when you are work, work is work. New relationships are even tougher since you and your significant other are trying to spend as much time together as possible. Just be sure to not hang around or let your significant other hang around your respective workplaces. You might think that nobody is noticing but it doesn't take very long for your peers, coordinators and leaders to figure out that your relationship is impeding the operation of your area. Don't be afraid to tell your significant other that you will meet up with them later. If they truly care about you, they will not distract you at work. Just wait until the shift has ended for the day and then go spend time together.

Have a Magical Time

I know you want to spend time with your beau. Who doesn't enjoy spending time with a loved one or a new relationship? Especially when the relationship is new, it almost feels like a honeymoon type of period. Well the Disney parks and restaurants can be a romantic setting in addition to being a magical place to spend time with your beau. Snuggling up together while watching one of the amazing fireworks shows is a great way to end a night together. Maybe attending a dinner show at Hoop-Dee-Doo Musical Review at Fort Wilderness Camp Grounds is more your pace? I love taking my fiancé to places like Citricos in the Grand Floridian resort. Or there are places like Boma at Disney's Animal Kingdom Lodge or even Ohana at the Polynesian Resort. All are great and some locations have seen marriage proposals as well. At Be Our Guest restaurant in Fantasyland, Magic Kingdom, there is something amazing about dining in Beast's Castle. And it is the only location in all of Magic Kingdom to have a beer or wine. You do have to be dining during the dinner time to order these beverages. I have also witnessed one Guest propose to his girlfriend in the ballroom. The point is that there are plenty of places to go with your boyfriend or girlfriend and enjoy time together in a Disney setting. Who knows? You may even one day be getting married at the Disney Wedding Pavilion? Okay maybe that seems a bit farfetched but you just never know!

A Serious Topic

There is also one more topic in this section that I feel needs to be addressed. It is a very serious topic and some may even consider this topic extremely taboo but it does exist at times. Sometimes Cast Members fall for their direct leaders and vice versa. In workplaces outside of Disney, maybe this is not a big deal. But since you work in an area that has a lot of other Cast this is a potential hot bed of rumors and innuendos if you are looking to cross that line. You as a College program Cast Member need to avoid this situation as much as possible. The ramifications of having a relationship with one of your direct leaders can lead to devastating results. Where you might not have any immediate consequences to contend with, the leader will for sure. They might get moved or they might lose their job entirely. They would be at the complete mercy of human resources on this topic. I'm warning you now; do not get involved with a direct leader of yours. Your peers are very in tune with what is going on in the area. The last thing you need is to be the focal point of rumors and accusations not to mention the stigma that follows you whether you stay at Disney or not. Some of you could be so bold to say that you are good at hiding things from others or even being sneaky when you need to be but just understand like I have said so many times before: someone is watching. Someone is always watching. This could be another leader, another Cast Member, one of the thousands of security cameras on property. Thinking about going with your secret love to someplace away from property? Think again! There are thousands of Cast Members employed year round at the resort. Good luck trying to not run into someone that knows you, your significant other or recognizes you both from work.

I can recall a few situations over the years where a CP and a leader crossed the line. A couple of them were married at the time (not to each other). And word spread like wildfire once their relationship came to light. But there was one situation that I recall that absolutely floored me. There was one former leader that was so smitten with his College Program Cast Member that he made a big production about proposing to her. It caught all of his other Cast Members by surprise, rumors of favoritism and worse began to surface not only in his area but every area surrounding the workplace. Inevitably, he was moved and shortly thereafter was terminated from the company. I consider it a crazy situation and a completely tragic and avoidable situation.

Chapter 9
The Reality of Your Program

Wow! What a week you have had! You have a new place to live for the next few months. You have made some new friends in your apartment complex, classes and training. You have even worked hard in your area and have had a chance to unwind after spending some quality time training in your work location. It sure was fun to hang out with your new friends and visit the park, water parks, shopping or whatever you chose to do. This is the fun you're recruiter probably spoke of or a glimpse of what you saw in the pictures and videos you've been shown. But hold on a moment! Did you sign up because it looked fun or did you sign up for another reason? Is this program going to give you college credit if you are still in school? Or are you already a college grad and trying to decide what to do with your life?

Regardless of your answer, understand that Walt Disney World is the busiest destination in the world that is open seven days a week, 365 days a year. It is a business...a business that you are now a part of. The Guests that come to the parks and resorts comprise of: Annual Passholders, locals, families who save up their whole lives to come one time, foreign tourists, domestic tourists and other Cast Members. Without these people patronizing the parks, there would be no need for college program Cast or anyone for that matter. It takes people who are properly trained to keep the parks, resorts, transportation, food, merchandise, events and shows running. So what does this have to do with you?

Don't Get Caught Up In Attendance Issues!

Let's talk about attendance. Attendance is one of the reasons College Program Cast fail their program. It's sad but true and very much controllable. Attendance at work is a requirement in order for the business to be able to run efficiently and effectively. When you do not come in to work, you are hurting the business. For those Cast that treat their program like a vacation, give away shifts and call out when they have something better to do, tend to fail their programs. When you are in the early days of your program, you receive a packet of information. Inside this packet contains important information about where you live, bus schedules, rules for your program and an attendance matrix. During your area training, you also work closely with an area trainer and/or leader and go over the attendance matrix. You will want to make sure that you pay very close attention to the days that cover the attendance matrix. Make sure that you have your questions clarified. Consider this (at this point) the most important topic concerning you and your program. I understand that it can be a boring topic but consider this some of the most vital pieces of information that you will learn from your leaders. You will thank me later for that advice!

For the most part, the attendance matrix is the same for most lines of business. It is based off of the Full Time Union Contracts ratified by the various unions on property and the Walt Disney Company.

How does this matrix look?

Here is the attendance matrix as it is seen on the union website in the document entitled: **AGREEMENT BETWEEN WALT DISNEY PARKS AND RESORTS U.S. AND THE SERVICE TRADES COUNCIL UNION(REGULAR FULL TIME) EFFECTIVE March 30, 2014.**

On **Page 27** of this contract it states:
SECTION 8. ABSENTEEISM AND TARDINESS STANDARD
Absences: Beginning with 3 in any 30 days = reprimand, Beginning with 6 in any 90 days = reprimand, Beginning with 9 in any 180 days = reprimand, Beginning with 12 in any 365 days = reprimand
Tardiness: A tardiness of more than two (2) hours will count as one (1) absence. A tardiness of two (2) hours or less will count as one-half (1/2) an absence.
(a) Procedures:

(1) The following items shall not be counted as absences: a) Work incurred injuries and subsequent related absences. Employees must provide supporting medical authorization which satisfies the Company in this respect; b) Medical leaves; c) Release of shift for medical reasons; d) Scheduled personal leaves where the Company agrees in advance to the leave; e) Subsequent consecutive call-ins for the same illness or injury will not count as an additional occurrence; f) The first six (6) call-in/call sick notations for employees who meet the following criteria: (1) The employee has one (1) or more years of seniority; (2) The employee must not have received attendance discipline in the prior twelve (12) months.

(2) An employee's failure to notify the Company of his/her absence a minimum of thirty (30) minutes prior to the start of his/her shift shall be recorded as a No Call No Show. "

The full contract can be found on the internet at the union website: **http://www.uniteherelocal362.org/wdw-ft/** and more specifically at: **http://www.uniteherelocal362.org/wp-content/uploads/FINAL-2014-FT-STCU-CBA-2.pdf**

Why do you need to know this information? This is the information that governs your attendance requirements. Be sure to ask questions of your leaders and clarify. College Program has slightly stricter rules than a full time Cast Member has and the company can alter these rules periodically based on business needs. Read through your packet and training information thoroughly. It could mean the difference between having a successful college program and having to explain to your friends and family back home why you were sent home early. Talk about awkward.

VERY IMPORTANT: Under no circumstances should you ever blow off a shift. What do I mean by this? In other words: if you can't make it for your shift, make sure you call Cast Deployment and call out. And for heaven's sake, make sure you call more than thirty minutes before your shift. Look back at the previous mention in the contract. Specifically look at procedure #2. (2) An employee's failure to notify the Company of his/her absence a minimum of thirty (30) minutes prior to the start of his/her shift shall be recorded as a **No**

Call No Show. "No call no shows are bad. They are really really bad. Three in a row means you are no longer in the Disney College Program kind of bad. If extenuating circumstances exist around you being able to make it in for a shift, you must communicate with your leadership team via Cast Deployment as soon as possible. Also Procedure #1 section e and f will most likely not pertain to you. Don't forget you are a College Program Cast Member. Your program is short and not all guidelines are in effect for you. Be sure to once again ask your leader for clarification for rules governing your specific program.

Is this all that you will have to concern yourself with? Not at all. But that's why I have written this out for you. If you are able to grasp the concept of common sense, you will do just fine. Pay attention to safety hazards. Report them whether you are able to correct them or not. The company prides itself on fostering a safe work environment. Not only safe from hazards but also safe from such matters as hostile attitudes and basic personal safety. Working with a widely diverse Cast means that you will be introduced to customs, cultures and nuances that are unique from your own. I would highly recommend that you embrace this as a learning experience. You will have ample opportunities to learn from your peers and leaders. The knowledge of different cultures is extremely valuable whether you remain with Disney after your program or go into the "real world" and work elsewhere.

Safety:
I have mentioned before that Florida is hot. And if you are not used to it, you will want to be careful to stay hydrated. If your area has to call a paramedic more than once because you have become dehydrated, this could be a problem for you. The company is relying on you to be available for your scheduled shift. If you aren't available to work, others have to pick up the workload you have left behind. Be careful. If this becomes a chronic issue for you, you might have to ask yourself whether you should continue your program. Look at the parks. Most of the work locations are outdoors. Transferring to another area because you don't like it or can't handle the heat of the

summer is virtually non-existent. Be smart about how you handle your program. What you put into it is what you get out of it.

Make sure that you are wearing a proper fighting costume. No need to offend a Guest because you decided to grab a costume two sizes too small. Also you want to be able to move comfortably if you happen to be working in an outdoor location. Purchase stage approved comfortable shoes but also consider wearing a shoe insert like a Dr. Scholl's or some type like it. The parks are predominantly made up of concrete surfaces. Sure there are pads behind the registers and counter spaces and even at some attractions but working eight plus hours on the concrete surface will take a toll on your feet. And if you aren't used to walking around that much on solid surfaces, your first couple of weeks will be rough on you. Hang in there! Your feet will tough as nails in no time!

Depending on where you are assigned to work, you could be required to use a company vehicle. The type of vehicle varies but can be anything from a delivery van, a pargo (golf cart type vehicle), a wheelchair, an ECV or even a motorized cart. If you do not possess a valid United States Drivers License, you cannot operate a van or street legal vehicle. Driving these types of vehicles requires that a driver to be licensed and insurable. Without a driver's license, you guessed it, you are not insurable. If you are required to drive any of the aforementioned, it is imperative that you follow all safety protocol! ECVs and wheelchairs are in Guest areas and backstage. If you aren't paying close attention, potential accidents can occur at a split second. Do not go joyriding in pargos or company vehicles. It isn't just about Guest and your fellow Cast being protected from the vehicle but it is your safety too that you must consider. Also, while traveling on Disney property, make sure that you follow the street signs and speed limits. The property may be private property but the roads are still roads that are bound by the traffic laws of the Florida Department of Transportation. The Orange Country Police Department does patrol these roads on property and will pull over a speeding car if they find them. Play it safe! Give yourself enough travel time to work so you aren't tempted to drive over the speed limit. Racing to work so you won't be late could be a big mistake.

Sometimes things happen in life. When it comes to safety though, most situations are avoidable. If for some reason something happens in the workplace that causes an injury or a strain, make sure you report it right away to your leadership team. Even though Health Services is available to you in the advent of an injury, your team needs to know about your issue. Why is this? Anytime a Cast Member goes to Health Services, a record of the visit is recorded and reported to your area. Then it becomes an issue for your immediate leaders to explain what had occurred to their leader. But if nobody was originally aware that there was an issue, this task becomes difficult. Again, the company takes safety very seriously and so should you.

Theft

When it comes to business, there are typically two types of theft: internal and external. Internal, in this case, would be an employee of the company and external would be a Guest who decides to take something without purchasing it. When witnessing an external theft, be sure to report what you have seen to your leadership time immediately. They will then take the proper next steps. But really, this section is about internal theft from Cast Members. Now I know this may seem like a silly topic or nonsense that it is even in this guide. After all, this topic has absolutely nothing to do with you. Right? Well I understand completely, however sometimes good people get caught up in opportunity. Sometimes the rationale is that the company will never miss a dollar or five or twenty or a hundred. Well let's just put this possible thought out of your head forever! The company does look after its assets and not just money but product, food, services and even empty cardboard boxes. Yes...I said even cardboard boxes. If you need boxes to move, you must partner with your leaders and acquire a material removal form. This form must be presented to security before leaving the premises with the boxes. Do not take this for granted. As for money and any other tangible asset, know that there are cameras on property that you see. There are also many cameras on property that you cannot see. Protecting the magic is just as important as safety. I have lost count over the years I worked for the company where people thought they could just get away with taking a few things. But let me tell you, all it takes is one time taking something that doesn't belong to you and it could ruin your future. And it doesn't matter if you think you have some amazing plan to never get caught. One term in business that means giving people free or discounted merchandise when they are not entitled is called: Sweat Hearting. Maybe you've heard of it and maybe not. But this is still considered theft. If you fail to ring up (as a cashier) every item that a Guest purchases and knowingly place it in their bag with the intent on giving it to them for free, you have just committed sweat hearting. Even giving your discount out to people is a huge no no. Don't do it. There is always someone watching somewhere whether it is electronically or in plain sight. Remember: theft is stealing and stealing is a crime. Continue to do the right thing and you will have no issues here. Consider this a serious warning.

Have a Special Time Off Request?

From time to time, things come up and College Program Cast might be looking to take some sudden time off. There could be a chance that you could need some time off for whatever reason. We all experience a need for time off at some point in our lives. Family could be coming into town to visit or maybe even some friends. Or maybe you are looking to travel home to visit with family? Before you can up and leave, it is always recommended that you put in for time off requests through the Disney HUB as soon as you know when you are looking to be off. Your schedule is usually available a couple of weeks in advance. If the schedule is posted, it's too late to request it off directly. Things that cracked me up to the point where I wanted to laugh:

- College Program Cast asking for any holiday off because they "always spend holidays with their family".

- CPs needing time off to go on a weeklong or a two week long cruise.
- CPs needing to end their program early without failure because they need to be home for the holidays.
- CPs wanting a set schedule (preferably opening shifts).
- CPs wanting a couple of weeks off because their family is in town (usually around the holidays).

These are a few that come to mind immediately. They are all humorous because (as stated before) this is the busiest tourist destination in the world and operates 365 days a year. College Program Cast do not accrue seniority and Full Time Cast get first dibs on holidays off. Most FT Cast are wait listed because the company can't give everyone off. The business still has to be run! Believe me, I understand traditions but you will learn quickly that you will need to create new traditions while employed by the Walt Disney Company (specifically parks and resorts division). This isn't rocket science. It goes back to common sense. It takes people to run the operation. As a College Program Cast Member, you are vital to the success of running the operation.

Need an occasional day off for classes or a specific set of days off? In some cases, you will be assigned classes in your program. Sometimes they are a requirement of your schooling and other times it could just be a part of the type of program you enlisted for. Whatever the reason, these classes are important and your attendance is mandatory. Take comfort in knowing that your scheduler takes that information into consideration when creating your weekly schedule especially when they are required classes for your program. They receive the class information along with how many weeks the class is going for so this way you aren't accidentally scheduled on a class day.

Looking for a day off just because? Remember: as I just stated above, you will need to submit the request through the Disney HUB. Your ability to get it off is based on if anyone else has already asked for it off before you. Plan ahead. You will notice by now that this is a reoccurring theme. Try giving your shift away or exchanging with a peer. You will want to make sure that the person you are giving a shift or trading with doesn't give them overtime. Your leaders can explain how to do this in more detail during your training. If they haven't mentioned it, don't be afraid to ask your trainer or leader. Ultimately it is your responsibility to be proactive about a change in your scheduling needs.

In the unfortunate case of needing time off due to a family emergency including a passing of a loved one, you will want to contact your leadership team right away. If you have to travel out of state for a funeral, you could be granted some time away at no penalty but you will want to discuss the full situation with your leaders. Do not be offended if they mention that you will need to bring back an obituary or a funeral announcement. This isn't because they want it specifically or are looking to cause you grief. There are times that the company requires this information for their records especially when it comes to attendance and or pay. Your area leaders will leave you to grieve in your own way just be sure to follow any instructions that they give you as well.

Memories That Will Stay With You a Lifetime

Do take photos and document your program as you see fit. BUT BEWARE! Under no circumstances should you use social media (Facebook, Twitter, Instagram etc) as a forum to sound off your displeasure with your roommates, coworkers, other CPS, leaders, the company or anyone affiliated with the Walt Disney Company. But you say that it's your right to do what......STOP. Let me stop you right there. Once you sign up for the program, you agree to conduct yourself in a professional manner. Actions that can be detrimental to others, yourself or the company are potential grounds for release from your program. Be smart about your program. Use common sense. Social Media is not your playground when you are working for a high profile company let alone pretty much any company nowadays.

Did you call out sick and just post status updates and photos from your park play day with your roommates or friends? Or maybe you went out partying in downtown Orlando while you were supposed to be at work. Don't do it. You have just set yourself up for a possible disaster in your program. Not only do you lose credibility with your peers and leaders but you may have also just violated a few policies that the company has set forth. My suggestion: don't be an idiot here. Read the rules of your program. These guidelines will help keep you from falling into an easy trap for yourself. Once entered, these traps are very difficult to overcome and more often than not, the CP Cast Member ends up being separated from their program.

Do you have a friend or roommate that is falling into this category? It is almost your duty now to at least warn them of potential dangers. There isn't any need to nag them. They are an adult too. At least you can rest easy knowing that you made an effort to rescue a wandering Cast Member from the abyss of program violations. Play it safe! Plan your play time around your schedule and PLAN AHEAD.

Also, try not to ruin the magic for others! If you happen to be in Entertainment as College Program Character or if you know of someone who is a character performer, please refrain from expressing this verbally to others especially within earshot of Guests. And for goodness sake, try to not post about it on social media. Nothing angers me more personally and upsets Guests when an overzealous Cast Member starts blabbing about who plays what character or what is behind a boarded fence or what attraction they think is coming soon even though the company hasn't told anyone anything. Just stop it! If you're wrong, you sound foolish. If you're right, you may have just ruined the magic for several people who will in turn probably complain to Guest Relations about you. I shiver just thinking about that conversation your leaders will need to have with you. Okay, let me temporarily step off my soap box here.

Do feel free to share with Guests and friends any helpful hints about where to watch parades, which attractions have a small wait time, great places to eat, cool factual fun facts about your work location that are stage approved and most of all to have a magical day! These conversations are very helpful and brighten Guests' day along with their overall experience. Besides, isn't it fun to be helpful? I know that I feel good giving somebody practical advice such as I am doing here too! It's almost like the circle of life but different.

Coming to Work While Under the Influence of Intoxicants

Having an occasional alcoholic beverage can be a way to unwind. Especially after a long day, I will enjoy a beer but not very often. I'd say this happens maybe once a month. Maybe this describes you perfectly. Anytime you consume alcohol (you must be over the age of 21), your judgment does become impaired. And the degree of your impairment is based on other factors like whether you have food in your system, your overall genetic makeup and quantity you consume. The point here is you must drink responsibly. But let's take this a step further. Under no circumstances should you go to work while under the influence of alcohol or any other intoxicant. I'm not just referring to the obvious intoxicants either. I'm also referring to prescription medications that can inhibit your reaction time or alter your ability to use good judgment. All of these things previously listed have the ability to put you and others in harm's way. If your physician is prescribing you medications of this type, you will most likely need to call out for your shift. You will also want to partner with your doctor to submit information to Health Services if you are required to be out for a few days due to prescription meds. Do not take unnecessary risks with this. Play it safe. Failure to do so can have serious consequences which could lead to an immediate release from your program or worse. And note this type of release from the College Program is not a successful graduation. It is consider a failure of completion.

Don't Ruin the Magic For Others!

Playing in the parks and on property is a lot of fun! You quickly began to formulate what attractions and shows you enjoy the most.

Maybe you even develop a strategy for how to get to your favorite spots and out of there in record time in spite of the crowds. Maybe you have learned so amazing behind the scenes information about these attractions? When you hang out with fellow CPs, family and friends you might be tempted to share this new found information with them. Now I now I have mentioned this before but please look at the big picture of your actions. I can't tell you how many times exactly that I have been playing as a Guest and riding on an attraction and have heard Cast Members talking loud enough for me and my party to hear. "Oh yeah. You can see (insert spoiler alert here) when you ride this ride." It doesn't matter what illusion you are explaining off. The fact is that if I heard you clearly, the family with young kids in line near you probably heard you too. We all love to share our knowledge with others. In part we enjoy doing this because it makes us feel important because we have inside information on amazing things. But please watch what you say and how you say it.

There is also a very annoying scenario that Guests do not want to be a part of: hearing about Cast problems or what they got up to the night before. Think of a Guest's visit at Walt Disney World as escapism. They are escaping from their everyday lives (hopefully). They aren't interested in what is necessarily going on in the real world at that moment. Why is this true? Look at how expensive it is to travel nowadays. Airfare costs are at an all time high. The cost of gasoline is still higher than it was over a decade ago. Hotel costs rise each and every year. Then factor in the yearly rise in costs of admissions, the cost of food and maybe even the cost of renting a vehicle. All of these add up to some very serious hard earned money spent on the part of the Guests. I don't know about you but I am not interested in spending my hard earned money to go to a vacation destination just to hear others talk about how mad that they are that their vehicle is not working properly. Or even that people wish they were paid more money for their work. If I wanted any of this, I would save myself a lot of money and headache by staying home and watching the local news on television. Be mindful of your onstage conversations and body language. This where you want to avoid being on the clock and clumping with other Cast. Clumping, in this case, can be defined as huddling up or following other Cast and making yourself unavailable or unapproachable to Guests. This is a behavior that you really should be avoiding.

Working in a Park and Taking CP Transportation

You were picked to work in one of the four major Florida theme parks. You were even fortunate enough to get one of the locations you were hoping for! My favorite part of my career was working inside the two of the theme parks. This was an extremely huge thrill for me. It will also be a huge thrill for you too (assuming that you were picked for a park role). But you will need to understand that the parks are what most if not all Guests come to Walt Disney World Resort for. Parks can get busy at various times of the year and if they get too busy, the park hours can be extended at short notice. If this occurs, you may not have even arrived to your work location yet. Once you get through the security process of entering the park for work, SURPRISE! There's a sign that says your park has been extended by an hour or more. So how does this affect your shift? You will most likely be force extended due to business needs in order to serve the Guests. Sure this can be frustrating and tiresome but it is the nature of the industry. The Guests are what keep you in your internship and others employed. You will need to suck it up and head in to work. Now if you are stuck working well beyond the last pick up time for you College Program transportation, don't worry. You can call the afterhours line that is in your check in packet. You may want to consider uploading these important phone numbers to your phone anyway. An afterhours shuttle will be dispatched to your location to pick you up and take you back to your apartment housing. There should be no need for you to even contemplate staying overnight in a breakroom. Besides, they aren't that comfortable.

There is still a way for you to get home. You still have the option to call an afterhours shuttle if you are caught in a resort or non-park location after the last scheduled College Program buses have departed. Getting home safely is just as important as getting to work safely.

Resort Amenities and Your Free Time

You had a long day at work and one of your friends or roommates has a great idea. The two of you should go over to your favorite Disney Resort that has an amazing pool and exercise facility. Since you do not work in that location, you feel pretty confident that you won't run into somebody you know. This way you can run a few miles on the treadmill and then take a dip in their amazing pool. Hey maybe you guys can even grab a cocktail while lying out by the pool! Doesn't that sound amazing? Here is the advice here: DO NOT DO IT. The resort amenities are specifically designated for resort Guests only. To gain access to some of these places, Guests have to use their room keys. These options are not available to Cast Members unless you are staying in the resort and only during the duration of your stay. Just because you stayed there for a couple of nights back three months ago does not entitle you to use the facilities anytime you like. If you are caught using resort amenities that you are not entitled to, your area leaders will be informed. Depending on the severity of the situation, you could have your program prematurely ended for you. Save yourself the grief. Don't do it. It isn't worth failing your program over being able to sit by or swim in a themed pool. Consider yourself warned.

Be Nice To Other Cast Members

At some point or another in our Disney careers we come across cranky Guests. It is inevitable. Whether it is the heat, family stress, and lack of food in their system or just an overall stressful trip, cranky Guests do not have a problem letting Cast Members know how they feel. In most of these cases, you, being the amazing problem solving Cast Member that you are, find unique ways to better these Guests day and help turn the situation around for them. This has an incredibly rewarding feeling and then you tackle your next daily challenge. But on occasion, you come across a Guest who is demanding and belligerent. They want the world and feel entitled to everything under the sun. But wait! This Guest isn't a normal Guest. This Guest is a Cast Member who is playing on their day off! This type of behavior from a Cast Member is absolutely ridiculous and isn't tolerated. Under no circumstances should a Cast Member ever throw a tantrum or get angry at another Cast Member. As working Cast we have enough to deal with as do the offending Cast Member / Guest. They should know better than to take out their frustrations on another Cast Member. If this happens to you, make sure you report the situation to your leadership team. There were several times in my career where I had to send an email or place a call to a work location and explain to their leadership team what the offending Cast Member did. Make it a point to also follow this rule when you are playing in the park. If you really are having an issue, stay calm and follow the chain of command to try and reach a reasonable agreement. If you happen to be traveling in the parks with friends or family, the same rules apply. Do not let any of your party cause grief while visiting as your Guest. Their negative actions can have just as much of a detrimental effect on your program as your own actions. Repeat to yourself: "Be Nice, Play Nice" and you will be fine.

The Holidays and You

This sounds like it should be an animated cartoon short kind of like the ones we used to watch either in school or after school. Well it is an important topic that should be covered. Almost every College Program Cast Member had issues with working during the holidays especially if this was their first time away from home. Every CP will experience this in some form. If you happen to start your program early in the year, you will be spending your program at Disney during Easter and the Fourth of July holidays. Now I understand that not everyone celebrates Easter. This could be due to religious or cultural issues but a lot of Guests do. The resort tends to carry a small amount of product recognizing "spring". This product is sold during that season and tends to go quickly. Getting Easter Sunday off is not an easy thing but if you work at night, there are several churches in the area that have Easter service in case this is important to you.

The Fourth of July can be an incredible day to work especially if you work in the parks. The fireworks are second to none! Also check with your area. A lot of times your teams will do pot luck or even the Cast cafeterias are known to do a discounted holiday meal of some kind. I can recall one year during the Fourth of July that the Cast cafeteria had a ninety nine cent meal. It contained a hotdog, a beverage and some fries. Now I can't promise that this type of deal will be around during your program but you should check just in case. Take advantage of these events when you can. Remember we are trying to save money and stay within our budget!

For those College Program Cast that join later in the year, you will be working during Halloween, Thanksgiving, Christmas and New Year's holidays. Many CPs find this time of the year to work their program to be extremely magical AND extremely emotional. Halloween is a lot of fun! Wherever you are working, you will get to see thousands of Guests dressed in costumes. With the Halloween ticketed event at the Magic Kingdom, Halloween feels like it is two months long! You know you want to dress up in your favorite costume and go play on your day off in the parks. Halloween not your thing then? The decorations are adorable and it is festive. So take some time to check it out and take a lot of photos!

Thanksgiving is a holiday that I always remember fondly with the family while I was growing up. The food, the football games (both on television and outside) were some of the best memories I have. When I began working for Walt Disney World, I found it to be a bit of transition spending the holidays over three thousand miles away from my family. Fortunately, I had made friends here quickly and we all bonded together to create our own "Fakesgiving". This is the term I created for when my friends and I would get together and celebrate Thanksgiving on a different day than the actual day of the holiday.

But working on the day of the holiday can be just as festive too! Don't forget that everyone working with you are not with their family and friends so you have an opportunity to share your favorite memories with them if you so desire. Again, check with your work areas before the holiday. A lot of work locations will have pot lucks and sometimes supply the starters for Thanksgiving meals for the working Cast! My area used to buy, turkey, mashed potatoes, gravy and sometimes ham. Then our Cast would bring in side dishes and we would have a daylong party for Cast when they took their breaks. If for some reason your area doesn't have anything planned, check the Cast Cafeteria. They usually offer a discounted holiday meal.

Christmas time is a very festive time of year especially at the theme parks. Whether Christmas is a holiday that you celebrate or not, it is celebrated by millions of people and is a huge part of the Walt Disney World Resort decor and festivities throughout November and December. Christmas time is my favorite time and at the parks (not just Disney but also at Universal) is extremely festive and decorated beautifully! The parades are incredible with their theme, costumes and lights at night. If you are feeling down about not being home for the Christmas season, take comfort again in knowing that every park and resort has some kind of decorations or offerings that you can enjoy. This is extremely helpful! I absolutely loved going to the Grand Floridian resort and seeing the full size gingerbread house in their lobby. It even was set up to sell cookies and fudge! Holiday music playing on Main Street in Magic Kingdom put everyone in a great mood. Also, every park and resort has a decorated tree that is themed out for the specific location. Please Note: the week of Christmas through the week of New Years Day are the busiest weeks of the year at the Walt Disney World resort. That being said, it is almost impossible to get any extra days off than what you are typically scheduled for. You can expect to be scheduled on Christmas Eve, Christmas Day, New Years Eve and New Years Day. Once again, your work areas may have some fun things planned for you like pot lucks and the Cast Cafeteria is a good place to go for a possible discounted holiday meal. Sometimes the Cast will even start up a Secret Santa amongst themselves. It isn't mandatory to sign up or participate but it can be fun if you enjoy celebrating the Christmas season. Along the same lines as Thanksgiving, my friends and I would celebrate with a Christmas dinner days before the holiday. I called it...you guessed it... "Fakesmass Dinner". It's just as a way to keep the humor up during the busy and slightly stressful holiday season.

All joking aside, the holidays at the end of the year come and go so quickly that you will actually be quite surprised how fast you see the New Year. Enjoy this time as best as you can and immerse yourself in the Cast activities. Once you see the castle light up for the holidays, you will begin to feel just how festive the parks can be. Did I forget to mention that World Showcase at Epcot has a different decorated tree in each land and other fun surprises?

Chapter 10
Career Development

This topic is near and dear to my heart. Career growth is important to many people who join the Disney College Program. Career Development is available to all Cast Members regardless of status. I spent a lot of time during my eleven plus years helping Cast Members achieve their career goals whether it was with Disney or another company. One of the biggest complaints from College Program Cast I have interviewed was that they didn't have any real solid information on how to develop themselves. This is one of the many reasons why I wrote this book. So here is some basic but solid advice on how to do just that.

Trust in Your Leadership Team

Your leadership team has a lot of resources at their disposal. Each of them started from an entry level point (possibly even similar to the one you are on). And they have had their own unique journey to get to where they are now. Never count them out as a potential resource or network. Start by communicating with your leaders. But let's take it a step further. Start by communicating with a leader who you enjoy working with. They will probably be the best asset to your future. But do not neglect your communication with the remainder of your leaders. It requires (in most cases) entire team approval for a CP to do projects or to be supported for other roles (when available). This start is called Starting Your Network. The objective to achieve roles that are project roles, temporary assignment, coordinator or even leadership require you to network and network often. The more people who know your name and your accomplishments, give you a better chance to land interviews. Notice I said interviews? Networking never guarantees a role and not keeping up on your networking could lead to losing opportunities for interviews.

Choose a Mentor Wisely

According to **dictionary.com**, a mentor is defined as: "a wise and trusted counselor or teacher." And having a mentor while in the Disney College Program is a very smart move. A proper mentor will help you with your resume, discuss your career path, establish possible networking opportunities for you and act as an overall guide through your program and beyond. You should be able to determine who is a genuinely caring and solid leader and who might not have your best interests at heart. A good leader will do what they can to find ways to get you introductions with others so that you can learn about the role you are seeking. This is why I suggest you start by working with a leader you get along with at first. Why would your leaders want to help you? Everyone wants to leave their own legacy whether they stay with Disney until the end of their careers or when they move on. By developing their Cast and helping them move on to the next level, leaders can look back at your accomplishments and show their leaders that they have successfully guided you through the next step of your journey. I was fortunate enough to develop several of my hourly Cast into Coordinators and a few of them became my peers as a leader too! Consider your communications and development from your leaders as a stepping stone to meeting new people and growing your network. If you happen to get a meeting with someone new or an interview, don't forget to send a thank you card. It's a nice touch and people appreciate the pleasantry.

You might even see an opportunity for an interview. How do I ace an interview? Well fortunately, most leadership teams will prep you on how to interview. They do this so they can also show that their candidate is truly the best and will represent the team well. Typically, you are put through a couple of mock interviews so this way they are able to give you advice on what you need to work on before going to a full fledge interview. There are also online classes through the company HUB along with books that can be checked out through the Disney Learning center. These resources are also very handy when you are looking to polish up your resume as well.

Remember: when your leadership team, interviewer or person you are meeting with gives you feedback, treat it like a gift. It is perspective on what you need to do to potentially get to the next level in your career. In addition to networking, timing is everything. If you feel that you should be a leader with the company as soon as your program ends, don't be surprised if it doesn't happen. Unless your next program is a Professional Internship, there is a process that Cast have to go through in order to have a chance at a leadership role in the future. So try your best to not show your disappointment if you are not chosen for a role. Disney career advancement doesn't necessarily happen on your time frame it happens on a Disney time frame. It can be a quick process or extremely slow and business / area needs will always dictate what happens and when. Also, your leadership team as well as the person or persons you interviewed with might be watching to see how you behave after you receive a decline. How you behave shows just how mature you really are and if you were receptive to the feedback given to you. Also, partnering with your Operations Managers is a great idea to gain more knowledge on how a specific area develops its talent. Besides, these managers are the ones that tend to make the hiring and promotional decisions for their assigned locations.

Professional Internships (not college program internships) are salaried leaders who are learning the ropes as Disney leader. They are compensated at a higher rate than a CP but are responsible for their own housing, transportation and professional attire. They do not receive benefits as a full time salaried leader would. These folks are all working towards being supported for the Leadership Casting Call. There is no guarantee of receiving a status position when their program is done. Several factors come into play for them. Are they supported by their leader? Are there any positions actually available at the time? The competition here is tight. The PI with support and has learned their role well might have a chance at getting into the leadership pole. Again, there are no guarantees.

Self Development is Important

A smart person understands that they are not perfect and should seek out knowledge on how to better themselves. Sorry but nobody is perfect. This is a key element on the journey of self development. So what can you do to better your chances of getting to the next step in your career? If you are determined to be a Disney leader because it is a dream of yours, embrace it. Just understand that you will need to work and work hard in order to achieve your goals. This should have been taught to you early in life. It is very easy to consider extending your current program but know that this will limit your availability to pursue a Professional Internship. This is the direction you should be trying for if Disney leadership is your dream. Again, make sure you let your leadership team and your leader's leader know about your goal. They will be the ones to ultimately support or not support you in your dream.

You should be meeting regularly with your various leaders in your work area. Learn as much as you can from them. Find out how they got to where they are. I refer to this as learning about their journey. Take the positive work habits of each of your leaders and make them your own. Every leader has bad habits...EVERY leader. Your goal is to not pick up on those traits or habits. Never allow yourself to get caught up in the drama of your work area as well. This type of environment is not conducive for promotion if you get mingled up in the drama. It is sad but true. To this day, there are people working in roles with virtually no chance of promotion. Why? They either instigated or participated in unnecessary drama that has left a lasting stigma on their careers.

Dust off your best business attire and make sure you dress for success! When going to a meet and greet or an interview, always dress for the role that you want and not the one that you have. Make sure you are in complete appropriate attire including nametag, lanyard and Cast ID. You only have one shot at making a good first impression. Should you wear a suit? I would say yes especially if you own one. If you don't, just make sure you are dressing professionally. Jeans, tank tops, flip flops and shorts are stating you really don't care about this meeting.

Need help with the Disney Look? You want to make sure that you are always in Disney Look when working. Do you have tattoos that are visible even with your costume on? Cover up that ink! You will need to use a professional grade cover up. Like to have an extra piercing in the lip, nose, mouth or other that can be seen outside your costume? Take them out! Have you noticed that all cast look clean cut and have naturally looking hair and styles? There is a reason for this. Be sure to read through the Disney Look handbook. Here is the source for the official Disney Look Guidelines: **cdn.disneycareers.com/managed/DisneyLookBook3_7_FINAL.pdf** Disney Look guidelines start on page 4

Network, Network, Network!

Also on that same guideline is the mention of the Disney Four Keys: Safety, Courtesy, Show and Efficiency. During your program you will learn in depth on how these four keys are a part of your everyday work life. Pay close attention to these basics while working. It is recommended that you articulate or are able to articulate how those four keys relate to your current role when you are at meet and greets and especially when you are interviewing. The people you are networking with want to know that you truly understand the concept and how they hold up traditionally within the company.

I learned quickly that networking was the only true way to achieve opportunities within the company. I made it a point to network early and often to be able to achieve my leadership role within Walt Disney World. One area of networking that helped me achieve my goals personally with Disney was by picking up extra hours in other parks and areas other than my own. The more people you meet and connect with, the closer you get to achieving your dream. If you work at Mouse Gear at Epcot, don't be afraid to pick up shifts at The Emporium (Magic Kingdom), Mickey's of Hollywood (Disney's Hollywood Studios), Island Mercantile (Disney's Animal Kingdom) Main Entrance (anywhere), Resorts, Parade Access Control (PAC at any location) or anywhere you can find extra hours. You never know who might be a potential decision maker for you when you try for a leadership role. When I first arrived in Florida, I was statussed to Hollywood Hills Merchandise (Tower of Terror, Rock n Rollercoaster featuring Aerosmith and Fantasmic). I picked up any hours I could find outside of my area. I was able to work all four parks, Downtown Disney (soon to be Disney Springs) and resorts. I worked hard and had fun with the Guests. I made it point to introduce myself to any leaders that worked while I was there. I began to see similar faces that helped me get moved from an extra hours shift in Africa (Disney's Animal Kingdom) to work at the Passholders Preview of Expedition Everest! That was so much fun!

When it came time for me to go through the Leadership Casting Call (LCC), I had worked for three of the four people on my panel interview! I was completely relaxed and nailed the panel interview. I then received a call within a couple of weeks and was placed into the leadership pool. I didn't have to wait very long for my first Temporary Assignment either. I was picked up by Mickey's of Hollywood as a leader within a couple of months after that call.

I am so passionate around Cast Development or really the development of others in general that I have included information for you at the end of this book if you require more guidance. But for now, read on and I will cover more on this later.

Chapter 11
Uh Oh! I Have a Mandatory Housing Meeting!

Sometimes Housing Meetings Need to Happen

You could receive an email or a physical memo requiring you and or your roommates to go to a mandatory housing meeting. First, don't panic. Take a deep breath and read all of the correspondence sent you or to the house. Just know that mandatory housing meetings can be for anything. Maybe it's an issue you are aware of. Or it could possibly be due to roommates fighting with one and other and you weren't even aware. If your College Program Housing needs to movie you and your roommates due to a facilities issue, this is another way to gather everyone together to facilitate the intended action. But realistically, it could be for anything.

From time to time, your apartment can be subjected to random inspections. This is done to make sure that nobody is breaking any of the housing rules or guidelines. If you haven't participated in anything illegal or know of any illegal activities going on in your apartment, then you should be alright. HOWEVER, you will be living with other people that you may not know or be familiar with. It is a good idea to pay attention to what goes on in your dwelling. If illegal substances are found in an apartment and nobody knows who they belong too, the odds are good that all members of the household will be let go from their program and possibly talking to local authorities. So do not bring any illegal substances into your College Program Housing. Make sure you report any such materials to your housing security and housing office as soon as possible. Protect yourself from violations this way you don't have to go through the embarrassing process of explaining later to your family and friends about what happened.

If you live in a wellness apartment, you will need to pay attention as to what is going on closely in your apartment. Since the drinking age is for adults that are twenty one and older, it is imperative that you report any underage drinking to housing security right away. If you are under 21 and caught with alcohol, you will be let go from the program and possibly seeing legal repercussions coming your way. And under no circumstances should you (if you are over 21) be supplying minors with alcohol either. This is straight up illegal and will land you into many legal problems including dismissal from your program. I've seen this extremely sad and abrupt ending happen to CPs who decide to go wild.

Should You Ignore Your Shift?

Your first reaction might be to just go to the meeting and forget about everything else. Maybe you are more inclined to call home and talk out the possible issues with the family or friends? Isn't there anything more therapeutic than hearing from a friendly voice to talk the day and night away about your troubles? At least you have that chance to get the problems off of your chest and maybe even get a better night of sleep. You can always just call your work area maybe the next day or two and everything will work itself out. Won't it?

Wrong!

Communicate! Communicate! Communicate! This is very important. If your housing office requires you to come in for a mandatory meeting and it occurs during your scheduled shift, call the Cast Deployment line right away! The phone number is in your packet and you will need it if you ever need to call out sick. The key to staying out of attendance trouble in this scenario is to communicate with your leaders. If you fail to show for a mandatory housing meeting, the company will most likely end your program and require you to vacate your apartment within twenty four hours. You will be given a form to give to your leaders stating that you are required to attend this mandatory meeting. If you get the form days in advance before your meeting, make sure to bring that to your area right away. This should help relieve you of the stress of having to call in the day of. Your leaders will be happy to let you know if there is anything else required of you before the meeting.

Don't Make a Simple Situation Into One Incredibly Challenging One

If you are the type that likes to approach every situation aggressively, I would try very hard to show restraint in this situation. In other words: don't complicate things! Make sure that whatever the issue is, that you cooperate fully. Tell the truth and communicate with your leadership team if your schedule will be affected by this meeting. The housing office will provide you with proper documentation for you to bring to back to your area. There is nothing stopping you from blabbing to others about your apartment drama but do you really want to invite others into any potential mess? People tend to enjoy listening to other people's drama but is this really helping you? I guess if you also prefer living in drama-land, then have at it. I personally prefer to live in a drama-free zone. I can recall thousands of times I've told my cast "when you clock in, leave your drama at that door." Unfortunately, I have worked in a few areas that are a hot bed of unnecessary drama.

Now problems can arise from time to time amongst roommates. It happens when you live with people you don't know very well and they don't know you. The company has a zero tolerance on bullying. If you bully or are being bullied by your roommates, remember that reporting the issues goes both ways. I have seen people termed for unnecessary drama that they have created or allowed to fester in their apartment. Everyone on the college program is an adult. Adults need to behave accordingly. It is one thing to have fun and enjoy yourself but it is another when people are being ridiculed, brunt of jokes or even harassed for being different. Embrace the diversity that is your peers. You will find that it is truly a learning and growing experience for all involved. And under no circumstances will violence be tolerated. Anyone who participates in fighting, acts of violence or vandalism can be subjected to legal and civil penalties. Think before you act. Seriously, violence is never the answer to resolving problems while working as a College Program Cast Member.

Chapter 12
Is There Anything Else You Need To Know?

Committees

The company wants its Cast Members to be actively engaged in their work area. This helps build a strong team. Each area has tools or plans set aside to help facilitate these interactions. But there are times when teams decide to refresh or relook at the way their areas could improve. And the more that active Cast Members participate in process, the stronger the chance of finding new and innovative ways to deliver better Guest Service and establish new efficiencies. To do this, however, there are times when various committees need to be formed locally. A committee could be formed over any number of topics. Typically, each area has a safety committee, recognition committee and a magical moments committee. There could be additional depending on your line of business but these tend to be the more common ones.

Safety Committees are usually established through a process that involves a union representative. College Program Cast Members are usually not a part of this type of committee. But in my experience, they can be involved with recognition and magical moments. Both require you to think about unique ways to have fun with your peers and have fun with the Guests. I know that I liked to get my Cast involved by not only collaborating with each other but also by creating the meeting's agenda and scribing for the meeting. The more engaged they were with our meetings; the more unique ideas were brought to light and created. If either of these two interests you, partner with your area leaders to learn about how you could be able to be involved.

Flex Your Creativity

Maybe taking notes at committee meetings aren't your favorite thing to do. Are you more artistically inclined? Not everyone has the talent to draw or design but there are some CPs who do! Every time there is local Cast Recognition event in your area, there is a potential opportunity to flex your creativity. I can attest that I thoroughly appreciated my Cast for their talents. Each time I facilitated or was a co-facilitator in Cast Events, I welcomed Cast decorative ideas and designs with open arms. I was blessed with working with some very talented people over my tenure. One Cast Member was so talented that I allowed him to design and create our area birthday and anniversary recognition boards. Each month he created them with a unique theme that the other Cast absolutely loved! These themes were more often than not about a specific animated film or action film. Sometimes time was of the essence and he would have to work quickly in order to complete these monthly projects. But when he did, everyone was impressed! And if art or graphic design is a field of study for you, wouldn't this help enhance your abilities or at least keep them fresh? There is a whole group called Communications that work on signage for events and on occasion have had a Professional Internship offered though the advanced Professional Internship website. So if you are a graphic designer, you could look into this as a potential future opportunity.

Avoid Conflicts of Interest

Although conflict is a part of life, certain types of conflict are completely avoidable. When you sign on as a College Program Cast Member or even as a full time, part time or seasonal Cast Member, you agree to avoiding conflicts of interest. A conflict of interest, as defined by **dictionary.com**, is "the circumstance of a person who finds that one of his or her activities, interests, etc., can be advanced only at the expense of another of them." And conflicts can arise at different stages for Cast Members when they aren't careful. The most unlikely for College Program Cast but still noteworthy is working for the competition. Since you will already have a full time schedule and most likely have some classes to attend, you won't fit into this category. But I can recall a couple of times during my almost twelve years with the company that a CP had picked up a part time job working with Universal or Sea World. If you are trying to balance this virtually improbable situation, you must be cautious to not work that second role in the exact same line of business. This is especially true for non College Program Disney Cast. To do this would place you in a direct conflict of interest. You will want to read your current program's packet of rules. There is a strong possibility that even working anywhere else during your internship is forbidden. You are required to have full availability even though you may get a day off for classes. Remember: I did mention that the program rules could change from year to year.

Who doesn't like saving money? Anytime I am able to clip a coupon before I go shopping, I become happy since I am saving money. Discounts are a shoppers dream. And having a discount to purchase merchandise in the theme parks is extremely helpful. As a College Program Cast Member, you do receive this type of discount as a perk. There are also times that you could receive free gifts from the company as a part of your Cast Recognition. The one free gift that comes to mind is near the end of the year when every working Cast Member receives a holiday ornament which is themed out based on the current Cast Holiday Celebration. Of course this could change and become something else if the company chooses but it was always nice to receive a gift from the company when they gave them out. At no point should you even consider reselling your gifts or discounted purchases online. Cast Members are not allowed to profit from their Cast discount. I have seen people lose their discount privileges and in some cases lose their jobs because they were working with non-Cast Members to profit off of their purchases or gifts. Don't do it. Don't even think about it. It isn't worth being expelled from your program. Consider this your warning on this subject matter.

Behaving Properly Backstage

So you had a great time at the downtown Orlando clubs last night eh? Maybe you just hung out with a bunch of friends at a party instead? Well we all like to have fun and enjoy ourselves in life. How that looks exactly will differ from person to person. It is what makes us unique and diverse. But there is something to be said for what is good, clean and fun for us outside of work may be unacceptable for us to exhibit at work. You will need to come to grips with the fact that you will have to maintain professional decorum at all times both onstage and offstage.

Over the years, tours on property have come and gone. Just know that tours are incredibly popular with Guests and Cast. Really on any given day, you can see some type of tour or another in or around your work area. Granted they are much more prevalent in the theme parks but are always a possibility elsewhere on property. Many of these tours given to Guests by the company (for a fee) will take Guests into the heart of backstage areas. While in these areas, Guests are restricted from video and picture taking. There is a strong possibility that you could cross paths with these Guests while they are on their tour. You will want to make sure that you are within Disney Look guidelines and all smiles when you come across these tour groups. This a strong reason why you should act professionally at all times especially while at work. Think of it as another way you are able to preserve the magic!

I feel that I should at least give you one example to drive home the point here. So here is a scenario I was told about a few years ago: a cast member, who was on their break in a backstage area but not an approved break area, decided to sit on the ground and use their phone. They were also a smoker and decided to light up a cigarette in an area that is also considered non-smoking. She was reading her text messages and at some point decided to call her friend. As she puffed and chatted away, a tour group was being escorted by a tour guide close by. As they learned about the unique backstage area, the Cast Member on break began using colorful language (swear words) to describe how she felt about her previous night out. Unfortunately, the tour and tour guide were within earshot of her conversation and the tour guide made it a point to get the name, costume description and description of the Cast Member. The guide then went on to apologize to the group as they wrapped up their embarrassing presentation in that area and moved on to the onstage portion of the tour. Later, that Cast Member went back to their work location only to be called into their leadership office. Due to the gravity of the discussion and her lack of awareness, she was released from the Disney College Program the next morning.

Now you may think that this is a harsh punishment because she was on her break but she wasn't in a designated breakroom. Once Guests are in the vicinity, the game changes a bit. She was in a backstage area that became an onstage area the moment the Guests were escorted by a guide. This is a real thing people. I will repeat: when Guests are escorted backstage by a tour guide, no matter where that backstage area is, that area instantly becomes an onstage area. If you are in a designated breakroom location, you are fine. Guests do not typically get tours that involve your rest areas. Make sure that you only use your phone in those designated break areas. And for heaven's sake, watch the language! Guests aren't the only ones that do not want to hear a potty mouthed tirade. Your peers are trying to unwind and relax on their breaks as well. Keep your conversation to yourself. And as for smoking, you can smoke in designated backstage areas when you are working. Make sure that you only smoke in those designated areas.

You're at work and you suddenly need to use a restroom? Make sure that you use one of the backstage restrooms while you are working your shift. At no point should a costumed Cast Member enter the onstage Guest restrooms unless they are assigned to clean them. I have actually heard some Cast say that it is unfair that they cannot just use the restroom onstage near their work area. My argument is that the moment that they go to use the Guest restrooms in costume, they have shattered the element of show quality for Guests. Just take the time to figure out where your closest backstage restroom is and plan on using it when you need to use the facilities and you're working. There is no need to complicate this any further for yourself.

Celebrity Interactions

We know you love going to Disney parks and Guests love playing there as well. What about celebrities? After all, aren't celebrities people too? They may be famous but they have wants and desires just like everyone else. So why wouldn't some celebrities want to go play in the happiest place on earth? Well the truth is: some celebrities do go play at the house of the mouse. Anaheim might be a little different in how celebrities chose to play at Disneyland since it is really close to their backyards. But in Florida, some will go incognito and others will have a designated tour guide to assist them throughout the parks and resorts. These guides also help any unwanted crowd attention since Guests could be fans of whoever is playing. But as a Cast Member, you will need to keep the emotions in check. When you are on stage, you are to treat all Guests (celebrity or not) with the same legendary Guest Service you have been delivering all along. You should never ask any high profile Guests for an autograph or even a photo with them. This only compounds a problem that shouldn't exist. These celebrity Guests are here to play and escape from their everyday life just like everyone else. Now I know you might be thinking that if they are a celebrity they are fair game but you would be thinking incorrectly. You are working on private property and not public property. These types of guidelines are in place to allow everyone to have a safe and fun time regardless of status or fame.

And if you happen to be backstage when celebrity Guests are being escorted from place to place, the same rules are in effect! Do not approach them to say words of kindness or otherwise. Do not approach them for an autograph or to take a selfie with them. Besides, taking photos backstage are not allowed. Just go about your everyday business and then you can have a great story to verbally tell your family and friends later. So which celebrities go to the parks? Honestly there have been too many over the years to name them all. I have personally ran into (by accident), actor Gary Sinise. It was during the winter holiday and around the time that he was to appear at the Epcot Candlelight Processional. He was very nice and wished me happy holidays as I apologized for bumping into him. We were each heading around opposite side of a blind corner. And I did hold a door open for NFL Hall of Famer Brett Favre one time. Just use the best practice of letting celebrities do their thing and you will keep yourself out of trouble.

Here is one example that I had witnessed personally: a celebrity being approached backstage by a Cast Member (who was not working that day) and asking for an autograph. Disney's Hollywood Studios used to host an event called: ESPN: The Weekend. During those days, celebrity athletes would make an appearance and either be a part of live EPSN broadcasts or be a part of a question and answer panel on a stage built in front of the former icon of the park (the Sorcerer Hat). They would travel to the stage in a motorcade that would drive the length of the main entrance to the park to the stage and then back once their performance was over. I was working near the main entrance when I noticed one of my Cast Members heading backstage after a motorcade just exited. I wandered to the area to determine if anything inappropriate was taking place since there were several celebrities back there at that point. As I entered the backstage, I saw my Cast Member approach NFL Hall of Famer, Jerry Rice and as I walked up behind her, I heard her ask for his autograph. Clearly he was surprised by this since his body language suggested that he was looking for his tour guide as he reluctantly signed her football. BUSTED! I loudly made it a point to her that she was in the wrong by saying "I know you aren't bothering the scheduled talent for a picture or an autograph backstage? You know this is a huge no no." Mr. Rice was very kind to dismiss it as being okay but she knew that she had been caught and quickly tried to develop some story as to why her actions were justified. Once the rest of my team became involved, her program was ended and she had to leave. It's unfortunate but not worth losing out because of a silly autograph.

Are You a Mommy-to-be?

As I've mentioned before, everyone's journey through the Disney College Program is unique. Don't worry! I am not going to go through and explain to you about the birds and the bees. By now you should have already learned about that topic so let's move on. There have been a few occasions over the years that I have had female CPs come into my area and are with child. Good news for those College Program Cast Members that are pregnant. Almost every costume has a maternity option. The reason for this should be obvious but for arguments sake, let's look at the regular costumes. When I asked everyone of my former CPs how they felt about their costumes, the predominant answer from males and females were that the costumes can be restrictive in their movement. Now this is even after finding a proper fitting costume. Now I am not a scientist and I understand that every ladies physiology is different. But in theory, as a pregnancy grows, so does the waistline. Traditional costumes are unable to accommodate this type of growth and still fit and look comfortable. So maternity options were created to allow the soon to be mommy Cast Member to work as comfortable as possible. You will want to verify that you r area has that option for you if you are expecting.

Also, when you are expecting, you will probably be spending some quality time visiting with your doctor. Make sure that you communicate with your area when you have appointments concerning your medical condition. And if your doctor has any type of physical restrictions due to a pregnancy, you will want to bring that medical paperwork to Health Services immediately. Please understand that any type of personal restrictions your doctor places on you could affect whether or not you are able to even work your normal location. In fact, if they are so severe of restrictions, you might have to rethink whether or not you should continue your college program. Please take the health of yourself and your baby into consideration. Remember all of the times I harped on you about staying hydrated? You now have to stay hydrated for two (or more)!

Consider the timing of your pregnancy too. Are you trying to do a college program that has a graduation date near your due date? If so, you should seriously consider waiting and doing a program later.

You already will have a full work load and classes. Do you really want to push yourself to fit this all in while still trying to get enough rest? Just the thought of this makes me feel exhausted. Just put you and your child first. You can always try again later. You can check with your recruiter if there is an option for a delayed program. I cannot promise that this option exists anymore but in the case of being pregnant, you may want to at least ask. Don't forget that even after you have your child, there always needs to be a plan on who will be watching your child. Unfortunately, childcare is not available to College Program Cast nor are you able to bring a baby with you on the program. Sorry. Four to seven roommates are not going to have the time or patience to watch your child either. Just make sure that you have a solid plan in place if you attempt a college program while pregnant.

Make Sure You Give Accurate Information to Guests

Depending on your role, you could get Guests approaching you with repetitive questions. Over time, you will grow accustomed to this and you will be giving these repetitive answers with a smile while you are wishing the Guest a magical day. But there is a chance that you may run into questions that you really don't have the answer or the answer you are about to give isn't one that you are completely confident if it is correct. When this type of situation arises, take the time to find the correct answer for the Guests. Do not guess at your answer. Here is an example for you: a Guest comes into a shop and is looking for a specific item. Unfortunately, your shop doesn't carry it. They ask you where they might be able to buy it. You are busy with a line of Guests and believe you have seen the item in a theme park shop but you're not completely sure but you decide to go ahead and let them know where they should go. The Guest leaves and goes about their day. They happen to come across the shop you referred them to. They are excited to finally pick up the item they have been looking for. They search the shelves frantically but find nothing. They ask a Cast Member in the shop but alas, they too have now told them that it isn't an item they carry. Uh oh! This is turning awkward quickly and now the Guest is frustrated. "But the Cast Member I spoke to promised me that you carry the item!" But you didn't really promise them. However they interpreted your confidence as just that, you are completely knowledgeable on the subject. This lapse in judgment has now spread to a new location and a dissatisfied Guest.

But you didn't get selected for merchandise so you have nothing to concern yourself with. Right? Well let's look at a different line of business. You are working at the main entrance, front desk or a resort, custodial, food and beverage or anywhere for that matter. A Guest approaches you and asks whether or not an attraction is up and running. They are excited to go ride it for the first time ever but it wasn't available to them earlier. You don't remember anyone on your team talking about any attractions being down so you go ahead and assume that it's currently operational. Your guest asks if you are sure and you nod as you continue working diligently. They head over to the attraction quickly only to be disappointed and distraught that it is still not available to them. Take the time and utilize your resources to get the correct information. There is no need to create a negative experience or an awkward situation for yourself or your Guests. Know your resources!

Have Fun!

You have to enjoy yourself and have fun! Isn't that the whole point of coming to the Disney resort? It is most certainly for the Guests and it is very easy to do for working Cast Members as well if you try. Aside from playing in the parks (which is obvious), you have plenty of opportunities to have fun with the Guests while you work! There will come time when your work location might be less busy than normal. This is the perfect time to liven up place! Grab those Mickey stickers and hand them out. Grab the bubble wand and watch the children have fun chasing the bubbles. Maybe your location does a trivia challenge? Or maybe it is just as simple as grabbing a Mickey mitt and waving to Guests as they pass by. You will not be chastised if you are actively engaging the Guests. This behavior is welcomed. If you are in a park, the early morning hours are a fantastic time to go out and have fun! Guests are heading to the attractions and maybe not stopping at your cart or shop. This would be a great time to step out from your area and wave while wishing them a magical day. The resorts have a different type of feel. Guests are eating and browsing early before they head to the parks so the opportunities for these fun magical moments tend to come about during the heart of the day.

Chapter 13
End of Program

The End is Near

This statement usually conjures up a picture of a man walking the city streets holding up a sign saying: "The End of the World is Coming!" Maybe even a guy ringing a bell shouting that previous statement. Okay, maybe I watch way too many movies. But there is a saying that all good things must come to an end. And no matter how much fun you have had over the last couple of months or even year, your College Program will end. It is a sad reality for many. But this is a good thing. Let me explain. Think about all that you have learned through the duration of your program. You have gained some skill sets that you previously didn't have or needed to enhance. You are now more alert to your surroundings than ever before. You have a keen eye for safety issues and have the knowledge on how to correct the issue or how to report it. You are an expert in your work area and understand your role better than anyone (hopefully). You are able to direct Guests to any location they are looking for in the parks, resorts or on property. You have the best two finger Disney Point of anyone you know. You randomly pick up fallen trash in competitors theme parks without even blinking an eye. You are now fully conditioned to be the best Cast Member or model employee for another company.

The reality of your program ending probably won't really set in until your friends or roommates start talking about it or if you sit and ponder it. Oh and trust me...someone will bring it up. It's a weird phenomenon but a sense of urgency starts to creep in near the end of your program. You and your roommates start talking about your favorite things that you have experienced. And during the last few weeks, you will start making plans to go to the parks and ride all of those attractions you love and go see all of those shows you adore. You may also be planning on going to some of the restaurants that you haven't eaten at yet or want to revisit. During those last few weeks, you will be trying your best to fit all of these things in while you finish out your remaining shifts. Remaining shifts? Oh my! I just said it! You only have a few shifts left. Go work those shifts and go out to the parks and take those last minute photos. Go out and and pose with your favorite characters at their meet and greet locations. Go grab that last minute ride on It's a Small World. Who doesn't love It's a Small World? I mean it is a small world... wait for it... after all. And yes I went there. Do that last minute shopping at Downtown Disney (soon to be Disney Spring) or even at the local outlet malls. The point of all of this is, you will be leaving soon and you should finish up any of your must do checklist now especially if you do not live in the state of Florida.

Graduation From the Program

So what is the objective or the point of even being in the College Program? Well I have basically told you in many words but here it is: **you want to successfully graduate from your Disney College Program.** People participate in the program for different reasons as we established earlier. Some are here for work experience and plan on taking their knowledge with them once they have attained their degree. For those that have already graduated from college, they could be looking to start their own business or just take their new found skill sets to a company closer to home. And then there are those people who joined the program because they have a deep love for the Disney Company and its rich heritage. But whatever your reason for initially joining is, one fact remains. You are nearing the end of your program and you still have a ceremony to attend!

At some point as your program draws to a close, you will find out when the planned Disney World College Program graduation day will be held. This released information will tell you not only what day but also the time, the location and dress code. Now I have never attended one of these ceremonies personally but I have seen plenty of photos from College Program Cast that have attended. Everyone appears to be dressing up in semi-professional attire. I cannot recall anybody wearing jeans, shorts or tank tops. Almost everyone has their picture taken wearing College Program Graduate ear hats with tassels, holding a certificate of completion and with a Disney character. There are usually snacks and beverages and a lot of peer to peer interactions. I have heard that this is a great opportunity to get contact information from peers that you don't get to see as often as you would have liked and a lot of people make plans for a reunion in the not too distant future. The overall event is incredibly fun but also incredibly emotional. I have heard of some graduations that have slideshows of CP photos in their work environment as well as when they were out playing in the parks.

But hold on a second! Did you remember to request the time off from work? You didn't just seriously show up to this graduation event and then take several dozens of photos. Did you? Oh no! You also posted them to social media apps while using hashtags and tagging your friends? This venue and event is treated just like as if you went to a theme park during your scheduled shift. This means you have just potentially created a bad situation for yourself when you have worked so hard up until now and have done so well! Well fortunately for you, this book was written to help you avoid such pitfalls or nightmares. The moment you find out when your graduation ceremony is, put in a schedule request on your Disney HUB! You are still responsible for making sure you get the time off and by doing so in the correct manner. Fortunately, the ceremonies are never scheduled on a peak holiday so there is no need to panic about it being on Christmas Day or Easter Sunday. The College Program group understands the concept of business needs and Guest needs. Understand that you may not be able to enjoy the entire day of graduation events but if you communicate your desire to go to the graduation, you will have an opportunity to enjoy some it whether it s before your shift or just after. As I have suggested many times prior in other chapters, PLAN AHEAD! Then go to the ceremony and enjoy it! You only have a few shifts left. Officially you are in the home stretch!

The Last Few Shifts

With only a couple of weeks to go, you are probably feeling mixed emotions by now. If you hated your work area, I apologize and feel bad for you. No area is perfect but I would have liked to think that you were able to find much joy working with the Cast and leaders in your area. If you really didn't enjoy yourself, you are in the minority of College Program Cast Members. Maybe you didn't put in any real effort? Remember something I touched on earlier? I believe you get out of your program what you put into it. SO if you put nothing into it, that is exactly what you are left with,

But realistically, you are in the category of College Program Cast Member that has mixed emotions because you truly enjoyed your experience. You found that not only where your leaders supportive, informative and helpful but also the Cast in your workplace too! You have spent so much time with them that it feels like you are with family. Well here is some more good news! They are now a part of your family albeit extended family. If you haven't already, you have started sending friend requests to your fellow Cast Members and maybe even some of your leaders. To this day, I am still friends with a majority of my former College Program Cast Members. You never know when you might need a business reference for employment opportunities. Your soon to be former workplace is a great resource for your overall network. Don't let time escape you without having taken some time to send those friend requests!

Now here comes some really important advice! **Make sure you work the remaining scheduled shifts you have.** You shouldn't have to ask for a schedule change on your very last day with the company. Most areas are kind enough to schedule you as a regular day off that day since it is check out day and you will be required to leave your apartment. I am highly suggesting that you work your remaining shifts and not call out or completely no call no show because you have not successfully completed your program until you have done just this. You need to work out the last shift and then check out of your housing. Then and only then have you completed your program successfully. If you need a review for your school (some schools require it especially if you are to receive college credit), your area has a specific review form that is used. You must request the program review within the time period established by your workplace area. You will only receive the review on your last day and if it needs to be emailed or faxed, your area will send it directly to your school for you. This is not negotiable. Understand that if there is a rule in place, there was probably a College Program Cast Member in the past that abused a privilege. Take the topic of attendance for an example. College Program Cast used to get the exact same attendance policy as full time Cast Members. Unfortunately, some unscrupulous CPs read online or heard from former CPs of ways to be able to beat the system and get as much time off as they wanted without being terminated from their program. The problem was so rampant that changes had to be made. It happens. Just be sure to finish out those shifts. You have worked this hard to get so close. Don't let technicalities spoil your fantastic program.

Chapter 14

What Should You Do Next?

The weeks of your program have absolutely flown by! You've finished your program or you are really close to finishing and have that moment of dread creep in. The end of your program comes just as quickly as the start of your first day of training. For some that was too quick. "What should I do next?" you ask yourself. Should you extend your program? Or maybe you should go back to school and get your degree? But wait. You could postpone your education and give this Disney thing a real try and maybe you can just make this your career forever? The answer to this question really depends on your specific situation. The advice I give will be broken down into categories. We will look at: you have already graduated and haven't finished your degree. And just for fun, I will throw in a third category: wild card.

You Have Already Graduated

The Pomp and Circumstance march! You get to toss your grad cap into the air and maybe even the watch colorful balloons drop during your graduation festivities at school. It is such a rewarding feeling of all your hard work culminating into your college graduation ceremony. This wasn't your exact experience you say? In any case, graduating with your degree or certification is a huge accomplishment! If you haven't really thought about, you should. One of my leaders explained to me several years back when I only had a high school diploma and it has been something that has stuck with me to this day. She explained to me that job positions that used to accept a high school diploma now need an Associate's degree. Positions that used to accept an Associate's degree now need a Bachelors degree. And lastly, Bachelors degree preferred positions now require a Masters degree. I'm sure you can imagine the next part of this new found knowledge. But the fact is, she was right! I needed to get on the ball. So I signed up for school while working for Disney full time and pursued something that had not yet been achieved in my immediate family: a Bachelors degree. It took me seven years to achieve the goal but along the way I did achieve my Associates first then continued on until I achieved my Bachelors degree from Rasmussen College. The point is that you have several choices in front of you now as a college graduate.

If your graduation was recent and you have only been in just the one College Program, you could consider applying for a Professional Internship with Disney. But if you waited until the end of your program to look into it, you are too late for the next available PI dates. You will want to keep a close eye on their website: **http://profinterns.disneycareers.com/en/default/** for sign up dates and requirements to qualify. Timing is of the essence for this pursuit since the amount of available internships is much smaller than the amount of College Program spots. Hopefully you have been networking and partnering with your leadership team. It takes their support and approval to just give you a chance to be considered in the interview process if you are a current CP.

But your first College Program was so much fun and you just don't want it to end. Does this sound like how you are feeling right now? Maybe you are considering working a second College Program? You could apply for an extension which could lead you to another area or possibly keeping you in your current area. You will want to check with the College Program officials to see when the deadlines are to apply for an extension. Don't forget that there are thousands of applicants that have been through the recruitment process like yourself. The amount of spots open could be based on how many applicants that have passed the process. Don't miss the deadline for this if you truly wish to extend.

Or maybe you are just looking to stay with Disney and try for a full time or part time role? I mean you have had an amazing time working here and many of your new friends are talking about doing this exact same scenario. This option will require you to go to the Casting Office (across from Downtown Disney - soon to be Disney Spring). Everyone must go to Casting at some point in order to be considered for long term roles. Being converted to a seasonal Cast Member has become quite complicated and is no longer a guaranteed option. The rules have changed so often that I do not feel comfortable giving any advice on this topic. The best or sound advice I can give you is to visit Casting before your program ends and then you should receive better information on what you need to do to be considered for a role after your program ends. Unfortunately, these rules change quite often based on the trends happening in the business. I'm not saying it is impossible to get a role after your program but it is much more difficult. You might end up on a wait list and will have to go home at first. This is probably a good thing since you will need to make arrangements to find an apartment and possibly retrieve your personal effects from back home.

You Haven't Finished Your Degree

Do not stress out if you are still in school. You may even be saying to yourself, "But I'm only a sophomore in college." If you haven't finished your degree yet, my advice is for you to go home and finish that degree! Take a moment and re-read the previous section. Sure the College Program is fun! Yes, working for Disney can be a magical experience overall but you NEED to finish your degree! Disney will be there once you have graduated. Many times I have had conversations with CPs around this topic. There is nothing more frustrating than speaking with my CPs and they have plans on extending to a full year; they want to also do a Professional Internship; they only have a couple of terms left but don't want to leave. You may have convinced yourself that you can go back and finish at any time. Right? NO! NO! NO! This argument has been heard time and time again. The odds of you actually completing the degree once you have paused your studies begin to drop dramatically. You have come this far! Don't stop now!

But ultimately, the decision is all yours. You can do whatever you want. Again, you are an adult and can make adult decisions but I am strongly advising you to go back to school and finish the degree. You can always come back for another program later or even apply for a Professional Internship...maybe even twice! Your education should be your number one priority. You can always look at Disney Leadership opportunities later if that is the journey you desire to pursue. Your experience that you have had is very valuable to you in any case. You now know how a major worldwide company conducts its day to day business.

If you are planning on "pausing" you studies to pursue a full time role with Walt Disney World, you will want to re-read the previous section. You will still need to go to Casting and know that there is no guarantee that any positions are currently open. In most instances, you will be required to finish your program and separate for six months or more before you can be considered for a role. Remember that program rules do change every so often before a College Program begins. But you might be thinking: "why can't they just keep me and convert me to a full time or part time Cast Member?" It doesn't work that way. Your position is categorized specifically as a College Program role. Roles are only created based on business needs and there could be a wait list for people waiting to get a full time or part time role in your desired area. Remember: When you are looking at a full time or part time role that isn't an office and technical role, you are looking at trying to achieve a union role. Union guidelines govern the process for how these roles are filled. Cast Member seniority then comes into play along with Cast being able to meet specified transfer guidelines. Stop into Casting and learn more about your options.

Again the advice here is to not stop your studies because you have allowed yourself to become engulfed in the Disney magic. Go get that degree! Walt Disney World isn't going anywhere (as far as I know) and you can always come back AFTER you have finished that degree! And once you do finish that degree, maybe you can apply for your dream role! It will most likely require you to have a degree just to be interviewed for it.

Wild Card

As a realistic person, I follow the philosophy that life is not black and white. There is a huge area of grey where anything is possible. And on rare occasions, and only if you have networked properly, opportunities could arise in the company. Opportunities like project assistants could become available and usually require a lot of networking with the right people to even be considered. Whomever you chose as a mentor, will probably be monitoring for these types of opportunities for you to apply for as well. You will want to check out the jobs available online through the Disney HUB. Make sure you are proactive and partner with your leadership team if you are looking to attempt to apply for any of these roles. Their support and guidance is a must to even be in consideration for these coveted roles. It is also helpful if you are applying for a role that aligns well with your field of studies. Try to avoid applying for several positions at once. Think about how it looks when you are applying for say a dozen different positions that all are different in their responsibilities and expertise. Your many submissions tend to send a message to your leadership team. What is that message? It is telling them that you really have no idea of what you want to do. Now when I say message, I do not mean a literal message. I'm speaking of a general though that you have no clue what you want to do. You most likely won't see anything come from your applications. You need to stay focused if you find your "dream" role. But why won't you see anything come from applying to a dozen different things? Since you need your leadership team's support, why should they stick their neck out or put their name out there in support for a Cast Member that isn't focused on any one goal? The role you're applying for wants someone who is knowledgeable as per the requirements in the posting and someone who will put all of their effort into the role and not someone who will most likely role hop once they get bored.

The practical advice here? Stay focused and network properly. Each role on the Disney HUB has a deadline closing date for the post. If you post after the deadline, your application will probably be declined. Timing is critical here as well.

Chapter 15
The Top 25 Reasons Why You Should Be A CP

My goodness! There is so much to remember! Okay, you have read a lot of information up to this point. So far, this book has covered a lot of (what I believe is) valuable information to you. There is a chance that some of you will be saying to yourself, "this sounds too complicated" or "there are too many things to remember." It's ok! Yes there are rules and things to remember but you can handle this! You are involved with a truly unique once in a lifetime experience! This guide was simply meant to be a reference guide for you to understand fully what you can expect to see. Again, everyone's journey through the program is different. And your journey will be too! I have seen Cast with incredible anxieties in their early days of being a CP finish stronger than they had even thought they could be. But after reading about the ups and downs, I feel it is important to see truly what the top 25 reasons (according to former College Program Cast Members) why you should be a part of the Disney College Program. For this segment, I will treat it more like a countdown from twenty five to number one.

#25 You Were Paid During Your College Program!

Ah yes! The joy of internships after or during college. Most traditional internships are unpaid. Think about the people you know or have read about. Somebody wants to work in the fashion world but needs to break into the business. What did they do? Maybe they took an internship with a fashion magazine? They need to gain experience in the field in order to be taken seriously if a position ever opens up. So maybe that previous statement is also the premise of dozens of movies and television shows over the decades but there is some truth in those entertaining shows and movies. But being in this program pays you weekly! Every Thursday (unless it is a holiday then you are paid on Wednesday) you get to see your hard work in the for of a payday.

So consider yourself fortunate that you aren't working for free. Bring on the money because it's payday time! So you didn't exactly make it rain 'Benjamins' during your program. It may even have felt like you were working for free at times since you aren't eligible for overtime pay or benefits. But remember that it is still more than what traditional internships get since traditional internships are unpaid. Besides, you are working for one of the largest publicly traded companies in the world! And you received weekly pay! Most companies either pay weekly or twice a month. You just happened to have chosen a company that pays you out every week. I'm just hoping you managed to save some of your money by the end of your program. Wouldn't it be nice to head back home with an actual savings?

#24 Your School Gave You Credit or You Were Able to Further Your Education!

Oh! School credit! That might mean one less class you have to take overall and a quicker road to your degree! Many schools give their students the ability to earn college credit while participating in an internship that correlates with their main field of studies. If you happen to fall into this category, be sure to follow your school requirements so that you are able to get full credit for your program. Again, if you need a performance review for your school, partner with your leadership team early. You will most likely receive the review on your very last scheduled day. By giving your leadership plenty of notice, they are able to write your review along with the several hundred others that they may be required to write (depending on how many College Program Cast are statussed to your area). Even if your school isn't giving you official credit, this program is still fantastic of an experience and looks impressive on your resume too!

Some CPs are able to take classes with partner schools like University of Central Florida (UCF). My stance on education is pretty straight forward. Education is important and CPs should embrace any opportunity to further their education. This also includes any classes that you are able to attend at Disney University behind the Magic

Kingdom theme park. Even a class on enhancing or writing your resume will benefit you in the future. Any educational opportunity that presents itself to you, you should consider taking that opportunity. Remember: the further you take your education, the better your chance of landing the dream role you want regardless of what company you try to work for.

#23 You Didn't Have to Do Large Loads of Laundry Each Week!

Ugh! Who enjoys doing laundry? Seriously? Laundry is a chore that most of do not enjoy but is a necessary evil so we don't come across as smelly and offensive to others. You will have to do some laundry at some point in your College Program. This is inescapable. Seriously, you didn't plan on wearing dirty socks and undergarments everyday did you? Well Captain Stinky, that is just plain unhygienic and gross. In addition to those garments, you will have some shorts and shirts and linens as well but not as much as you would if you lived back at home. You have costumes that you were able to check out, wear to work and turn in when you were done that day or that week if you wanted to. This comes in handy if Costuming carries plenty of your costume size. Smaller loads of laundry mean spending less time doing laundry. As long as you aren't having any kind of an allergic reaction to the costume itself, you can take full advantage of not having to launder your own costumes. Now I just mentioned "allergic reaction". There are times in the past when I have had Cast who had skin sensitivities when they wore costumes for the first time. To alleviate this issue, they usually took the costume pieces home and washed them themselves in their own laundry detergent. This proved to be an effective resolution for them. Just remember to take advantage of the fact that you can get those new costumes often. Don't get caught in the trap of forgetting to turn in your costumes or jackets when costuming requires you to. The cost of these are ridiculously high for a reason. The payroll deductions are so high if you check out a costume and fail to return to prevent people from keeping them as mementos. And when I say they are expensive, I absolutely mean VERY expensive.

#22 College Program Events Are Just as Magical as the Theme Parks!

Special events are just as the namesake suggests, they are special. They help break up the everyday workload and offer fun opportunities to unwind. Each College Program has a couple of events that are extremely fun to attend! You will want to make sure you put in your schedule request early if you plan on attending the entire event from start to finish. Your College Program Housing Office typically releases flyers to the CPs to inform them on when, where and what time the events take place. These are great opportunities for you to capture some great photos for your collection of memories to take away from your program. Just the graduation ceremony day alone is a spectacle unto itself! You get your College Program Graduation ear hat and your certificate of completion. Characters also tend to make an appearance and are a huge hit. There are also people there available to assist you with taking photos so this way you won't need to make every photo a selfie. Plus you may want to consider leaving your selfie stick at home. Disney recently banned the use of selfie sticks in its theme parks. It just seems like a good idea that you don't bother to bring it with you to the events either. I have also heard of a College Program Formal event. My understanding is that it has evolved into a end of year party that is sometimes at a water park, Mickey's Retreat or a convention ballroom on property. It is as it sounds though (depending on location) a place to dress up, dance, eat, mingle and take a lot of photos.

#21 You Mature Quickly Once You Are On Your Own!

Many people have an opportunity to leave home and live in a college dorm or share an apartment with friends. But then there are also many who do not. And some people do mature faster than others. But whether they attend a community college or just a small college that doesn't offer dorms, some have to live with their family while they attend school. We all want to be treated as adults but leaving home for the first time can be scary. But doing this is really preparing for independence and being on your own. The Disney College Program does force you to leave the comfort of the family nest if you were previously in that living situation. And you are forced to learn how to successfully live with others that have different habits from your own. If everyone has the same or similar type of work schedule, you learn the true meaning of the word compromise and your time management skills become enhanced. There is nothing more challenging than four to six people all racing to use the bathroom to get ready to start their day!

You are also surrounded at work by fellow Cast Members of all ages. You tend to learn quickly from the seasoned Cast about all of the nuances of your work location. Their knowledge is quite invaluable and they are more than capable of giving you sound advice when you are having some difficulties as well. Cast Members are fantastic when guiding or helping out other Cast Members. Think of them as one big family! Do your best to avoid picking up any of their bad habits though. But look at you now! You not only survived your program but you are stronger and more independent now! Way to go!

#20 You Gain a New Found Respect For Safety!

Safety is a word you have heard many times in this book and hundreds of time while at work. You have been through so many various safety discussions and training classes. You have gotten into the habit of paying close attention for any slip, trip or falling hazards. You have a keen eye for spotting excessive water on the ground and springing into action to clean up the mess. You pay close attention to how you position your body when lifting, pushing or pulling. You also jump in to lend a hand when someone is clearly lifting a load that is extremely heavy. Basically, safety has become so ingrained into your psyche that you react without thought when you see potential safety hazards even at your College Program Housing. You need a superhero costume and cape! You are Super Safety! Wait! What will my family and friends think or even my next employer?

Don't worry! This is normal behavior and it will last you for many years to come. Your next employer will be grateful that you have that keen eye for safety. You will be more in tune with slips, trips and fall hazards when you go shopping in regular stores, at home and in your future work areas. You know you probably want to pick up a pair of Shoes For Crews shoes before your program ends. They may not look fashion conscience but my goodness they sure are comfortable. Also, I have been away from the company for a few months now and I still have these muscle memory reactions when I am out at the grocery store or just walking around the streets of Celebration, Florida.

#19 You Appreciate Your Leaders Empowering You to Take Care of Guests Without Micromanagement!

It can be frustrating when leaders micromanage you. But just know that some leaders like to micromanage every situation. It is just the chemical makeup of their leadership style. It isn't a good style or bad style but just a style. But a lot of leaders do not micromanage and you will grow to appreciate having a healthy mix of both. The one thing that makes the non-micromanaging leaders stand out is that they will explain to you during your program what empowerments you have to be able to assist Guests. You should not have to deal with rhetoric or red tape to be able to replace a spilled beverage or a dropped container of popcorn. These items are able to be quickly replaced without having to call your Area Manager or the Vice President of your location. For one, that would be unnecessarily silly. And second, the Guests' time is valuable to them and the longer they stand around crying over say....spilled milk (yes I went there), the more time wasted in their overall experience. You will need to let them know how you assisted the Guest recovery after the fact if it is a basic situation. Unfortunately, if the Guest issue is more complex than a dropped churro, you will have to partner directly with your coordinators or Manager on Duty (MOD).

#18 Epcot is Your Favorite Hangout Now That You Are Over 21!

If you are not over 21, you will probably want to skip this one reason completely. Otherwise, ah yes! Oh the fun of going to Epcot and drinking around the world! Haven't attempted this at all? First, when consuming alcohol, please drink responsibly! Consuming alcohol will dehydrate you quicker especially when it is hot and humid outside. Be careful. Also, you need to know your limits! Know when to say when is how the saying goes. You still have to be mindful that you are a Cast Member. So going out and getting trashed in Epcot and acting a fool is not an option. You can go out and have a good time as long as you are behaving accordingly. And honestly, I have never been able to have a drink at every location in World Showcase. It would have cost me too much money and about three quarters of the way through, I knew I had reached my limit. Oh but did I mention that the tequila bar in the Mexico's Temple is fantastic? Their flavored margaritas are amazing! During the spring, Epcot has the Flower and Garden Festival but it has recently become a Food and Wine Light type of event. In the fall, Epcot has the Food and Wine event that is well worth the wait in the crowds! You will experience amazing food selections, wine and beers from around the world along with classes available for wine tasting that make the experience truly one of a kind. But my favorite spot that is a must stop every time I go is the Rose and Crown Pub in the UK Pavilion. I always buy a Black and Cider from the pub every time I go! This beverage is a wonderful blend of fruity with a bite. I have always preferred the sugary adult beverages and this one is tops on my list at this park. I found Epcot to be the favorite park for me to hang out in because it offered me an alternative to just riding typical Disney rides and watching typical Disney shows. Those tend to be overcrowded and a lot of children everywhere. Now it isn't like Epcot is children free or free from all of those beloved Disney attractions. I just find it to be a healthier balance for me. You might like Disney's Animal Kingdom, Disney's Hollywood Studios or Magic Kingdom better. But for relaxation in a major theme park, Epcot is extremely tough to beat for those people over 21 years of age.

#17 No Matter How Many Times You See a Character in the Parks, Your Inner Disney Geek Comes Out!

Characters are what the company was founded on. The timeless classics that we have watched and re-watched thousands of times. We connect with them in our youth and adulthood. These characters bring out the joy in others. You probably have your own favorite memory of seeing them as well. You have seen it many times by now just walking in the parks and resorts. A little child yells out to their family "Oh look! It's Mickey!" or really any characters name. They run up to get in line and give the character a hug and maybe ask for an autograph while their photo is being taken. The emotional response is real and so is yours when you see them. It doesn't matter if one of your roommates works in Entertainment or if you walk past the characters to get to your workplace. You most likely ignore these encounters because you are in a hurry to clock in and grab your assignment. But once you are working, playing in the parks or dining at a character location and you spot a character coming out to perform, you will probably regress to your youth and smile and even say the character name as you use your Disney point. Characters prompt a positive (hopefully) emotional response from our past. It reminds us of a simpler time when our imagination ran wilder than it does now. I did say hopefully only because some characters can appear scary. One CP told me that when he was five years old, he was deathly afraid of Maleficent because she was so mean to Aurora in the Disney animated feature film. Fortunately, he has no problem being around any of the characters now but when you're five things can be emotionally frightening. And even to this day, when I see Mickey Mouse in the parks, I still can't help but smile and want my photo taken with him. This takes me back to when I first went to Disneyland when I was five years old.

#16 You Appreciate Having Your Class Day Off From Work!

Classes are a reality to College Program Cast Members. In order to even be in school, you have had to at least began one class and be currently enrolled. And your school workload may have been quite heavy by taking five or six classes a term. While you were at school, there is a chance you had a part time job while going to school full time. Some people do this for extra spending money or to build a small savings while others work because their grants, scholarships or loans do not cover all of their college expenditures. But now you are in a situation where you are working full time and have a class or two that you need to take. Fortunately, your scheduling department has made it easier for you to attend this class or classes by scheduling you off for class day. This won't help your assignments finish themselves unfortunately but you at least have peace of mind that you have the time to focus on your studies and your homework. And you also learned how to manage your time wisely so you could complete those studies and make it to work on time.

#15 You Have a New Found Friendship with Carrying Around a Bottle of Water and Using Sunscreen!

The Florida sun, heat and humidity can hit you hard while you are outside. I know that I have mentioned the importance of consuming water and staying hydrated. And I apologize if this seems like I am beating this topic to death. But by the end of your program you will completely understand what all the fuss is about. One former CP explained how a Florida summer day felt during her program as: "It was like I was working on the surface of the sun!" Cast Members who work predominately outdoors are issued water bottles to use daily. And everyone including your fell Cast Members are counting on you to use it frequently and refill it frequently throughout the day. Dehydration is constantly a safety topic of conversation throughout the year. And with all of the available water refill locations in and around your work area, there is no good excuse for becoming dehydrated. Besides, water is good for you and a necessary element to your survival. Sugar drinks can taste amazing but don't forget that they dehydrate you quicker. This is a good thing to remember when you head back home. I actually lost a few pounds one summer from how much perspiration I had. I kept up on my hydration but even then it was sweating out of me almost as fast as I was consuming the water.

It only takes your first sunburn while working outside to realize that you really did need protection. Sunscreen or even (better) sun block will become your best friend. Protecting your skin is just as important as staying hydrated. Think about the worst sunburn you ever had as a kid. Remember how uncomfortable it was to try and go to sleep at night because your skin felt like it was on fire? And hopefully you didn't shift to sleep on your side. Ouch! You will probably begin investing in sunscreen once you go back home if you didn't before. Besides, it is so annoying when your roommates or coworkers clearly see you are sun burned and they all want to be jokesters and "accidently" touch your sunburned shoulder or hug you and slap your back. Ugh! Painful! Painful!

#14 You Cherish the Moments When You Are Able to Make True Magic For Guests!

"Does anyone have any Basics stories?" Or maybe you've been asked, "do you have any fun stories from your work day today?" Your leaders appreciate any stories of making magic for Guests that you might have. So here's a scenario for you: a frantic Guest approaches you in the park near the main entrance of Epcot. They need a wheelchair and are running late for their dining reservation in Germany. They are panicked and really do not want to even be waiting for the wheelchair. They are starving and rushed over from their hotel without stopping at their Concierge desk. You empathize with them and spring into action! You grab the closest phone and call the restaurant and talk to the Cast Member at the podium. You explain that your Guests are having some challenges and that they are running late for their reservation. The Cast Member at the restaurant lets you know that they will accommodate your late Guests and to let them know not to worry. You are able to hang up the phone after thanking your food and beverage peer and explain to the Guests with a smile that the restaurant will be waiting for them and to not worry. Suddenly you are being hugged and thanked repeatedly because you have just turned an incredibly stressful day for this family into the best day ever! So maybe that is a bit of an exaggeration but you would be surprised just how often this type of scenario and outcome actually play out like this. The fact is that you as a Cast Member have the ability to do many incredible things that make so much magic for Guests. Think of it as turning a Guest loss into a Guest win. These gestures not only help Guests but sometimes it helps them so much that they show their appreciation by letting your leaders or even Guest Relations know that you specifically had a positive impact on their overall stay. And when this happens, the stories behind the results stay with you as cherish memories.

One of the stories shared by a former Cast Member was about a time that they came across a child who was a huge Pirates of the Caribbean fan. This young lad was excited to become a pirate at the Pirate's League and to go watch the Captain Jack Tutorial after he was finished. He finished his makeover and went out to the stage but something happened! It was raining and raining hard! The show has been cancelled for the safety of the performers. Fortunately, the cast member was working at the Pirate's League podium and could see the little pirate coming back to the League. She knew that Captain Jack might be making a special appearance in the League since he couldn't perform his tutorial. She had him wait at the podium and verified with her peers inside and sure enough, Captain Jack was heading towards the League. She ushered him inside and had him wait while the captain made his rounds of hellos through the League. Before Jack left, he was introduced to the young lad and was able to take a quick photo with him. His mother was extremely grateful and he wouldn't stop smiling as he kept looking at his mother's phone (which she used to take the photo). This may seem like a small gesture but this was a huge moment for the young man. Making magic like this does leave you feeling extremely gratified.

#13 You Learn All Kinds of Cool Things About Disney and the Parks That You Didn't Already Know!

Just look at your introductory tour of your workplace on its own. Whether you are taking a tour of a theme park, resort or Downtown Disney (soon to be Disney Springs), you learn so much information about the history of the location, the heritage of the company and little hidden nuances that the average Guest just walking through wouldn't understand or maybe never even pay attention to! Then there will be times when you might be able to sign up for a discounted tour that is available on Disney property. It could be a backstage tour of a theme park or maybe even a tour of how the Disney Railroad operates. There are so many tours available that you could become a virtual Walt Disney World expert by the end of your program.

Also, your initial classes like Traditions will be so informative that you will probably be calling home to family or friends and begin sharing the fun facts that you learned in those classes. The point being is that by the time your program is complete, you will have learned so many cool fun facts and spotted so many different "Hidden Mickeys" through your journey that you will probably gain a new found appreciation for the resort and the company. You will have probably spent some quality time hunting down as many of these "Hidden Mickeys" that you have probably even learned about new ones that have been added well after the publication of the book by the same name was released.

Want to see some incredible attention to detail? Take one of the rafts out to Tom Sawyer Island at Magic Kingdom park. Many day Guests pass on this excursion in the park due to its lack of rides on the island. But there is so many cool details abound in and around the fort and the picnic area. Also, this is a great place to get a panoramic photo of the area near the Haunted Mansion and Frontierland.

Disney Springs, each resort and each them park (including individual attractions, shows, shops and eateries) tell a story. This story is sometimes missed by Day Guests because they are caught up or focused on getting from place to place with minimal wait. These stories are what you may end up picking up on and learning about. It truly gives you new perspective on just how much attention to detail is paid to these areas by the designers and Imagineers.

#12 Turkey Legs and Other Foods Only Found Here!

Turkey legs....yummy! All right, I know that the thought of the gigantic barbequed bird leg may sound gross to some but to people like me, I absolutely love them! One of my fondest memories involving turkey legs was when a friend of mine from Oregon came down to visit during the Cast Preview of the attraction Expedition Everest at Disney's Animal Kingdom theme park. We rode that ride about six or seven times in a row and then became hungry. We left the attraction and bought a couple of turkey legs. As we enjoyed it, some crazy wild birds began staring us down as we ate the food. I was concerned that maybe they were angry that we were consuming a distant relative of theirs. But nope! They were looking for a way to separate us from our tasty carnivorous activity. Once you've tried one and enjoyed it, you will be frustrated that any others you try outside of Disney will not taste as good.

Pineapple Frozen Whips...oh my. These are very tasty! There is nothing as good as this frozen goodie. And if you are a Disney College Program Cast Member in Anaheim, you have one specific food item that I have yet to have as good anywhere else as I have at Disneyland. The Monte Cristo sandwich is served at the Blue Bayou Restaurant which is attached to the Pirates of the Caribbean attraction. There is absolutely NO location in Central Florida that has that offering AND is made the way you make it. It is deep fried awesomeness that goes well with their signature Mint Julep beverage. As you go through your program, you will come across some food items like these that you will fall in love with and deeply miss once your program is over. But they are so worth trying (in my opinion).

Oh how silly of me! I almost forgot about the famous Mickey Ice Cream bars. If you didn't have an opportunity to try this at least once, you are most definitely missing out! There is something amazing about this vanilla ice cream dipped in a chocolate solid shell on a stick confection. These addictive beauties are only available on

Disney Property and they are also a delicious treat that you will definitely miss once you leave. Or maybe you prefer the Kitchen Sink Sundae from Beaches and Cream? This huge concoction is another fantastic dessert that is meant for sharing. You should attempt this once as long as you aren't allergic or suffering from any other major medical illness. There are also other sweet sensations available as well! The Confectionary on Main Street makes a rice crispy treat that is out of this world. And if you really enjoy them, you can buy the big ones in the shape of Mickey's head (plain, ear dipped in chocolate and all dipped in chocolate).

#11 Living in Florida is a Fun and Unique Experience!

Florida is called the Sunshine State for a good reason. With the exception of a couple of weeks early in the year, Florida's tropical climate means sunny days and beautiful beaches! If you aren't from a climate similar, you will see lots of lizards and geckos. These little guys you will grow very fond of because they eat the nasty bugs like mosquitoes and the unavoidable cockroaches that outnumber the civilians in this state. The only thing that you can't help is if their sudden movements or jumping scares you. They tend to hide at night but during the day they pop out and jump from everywhere. They are very stealthy but again harmless. You will also think twice about jumping into a lake or a creek unless you are sure that there are absolutely no gators around. And yes you could actually be driving on a side road and see either roaming chickens or even gators. This would more on properties away from Disney.

My favorite part of living in Florida is that I am able to wear sandals, shorts and a t-shirt almost all year round. The summer evenings are quite comfortable and even during the few weeks of cold weather. A simple long sleeve undershirt and a switch to jeans and closed-toe tennis shoes is usually more than enough protection from the chilled winds. Outside of Disney, there is always something going on whether it is local marathons, food truck events or even conventions make this a truly unique place to work, live and play.

#10 You Were Able to Be a Part of the Holidays / Special Events!

As I mentioned previously, the holidays can be a very emotional time for College Program Cast Members since they are away from home. And if you remember a few numbers back that I mentioned the Epcot Flower and Garden and Food and Wine Festivals? Well the holidays and events are well worth the wait in the crowds that hang out there. They tend to be extremely festive and can help brighten even the most somber of moods. Or maybe even the hard ticket events near the end of the year? Mickey's Not So Scary Halloween Party and Mickey's Very Merry Christmas Party are also worth the cost of admission! And if you can purchase your tickets at the Cast Store: Company D at a discount, that's even better! The experiences you have working any of the holidays during any part of the year will be memories that you will cherish for a lifetime. No other vacation or resort destination in the world pays so much attention to detail and offers so many magical opportunities like the ones you have a chance to be a part of at Disney. If your plan is to go back home after your program and choose to not participate in any of these events will probably leave you with regret down the road. Unfortunately, one of my former CPs did just that. She had such anxiety when working during the Fall Advantage program that she went out of her way to avoid the parks during the holidays except to go straight to her work area and then leave that she expressed regret that she never bothered to see the decorations. She looked back at the situation and wished she had just taken the time to pace herself and slowly stroll through the parks and take pictures at least of the decorated trees. Oh and if you happened to be working during the Fourth of July holiday, you have probably witnessed some of the best fireworks display you will ever see in your life. And the fact that Disney performs their Magic Kingdom Fourth of July fireworks on July 3rd and 4th, you have a pretty good chance at checking out the fun!

#9 You Have a Stronger Self Confidence!

There are naturally outgoing people and some that are a bit more reserved. Whichever type you are, look at how you are interacting with others as your program is coming to an end. Someone has approached you with a familiar question asking about the location of the exit or the restrooms and you are able to quickly grab a map or walk them over to the area since it is close by. You know your work location and theme parks better than you know your own hometown. You have endured some of the most intensely busy times and have been super productive during the few down times you have experienced at work. You need to take a moment and relish in the fact that you not only learned things but you have matured faster than if you would have avoided the program. You have endured negative Guests and have had fun with the many happy and excited Guests that have crossed your path. Way to go! You are officially a part of adulthood and have worked for a worldwide recognized company.

#8 There Are Many Fun Things to do In Central Florida!

Remember there is more to life than just Disney. And in the surrounding areas off of Disney Property there are hundreds of things to do if not thousands! Hopefully you were able to enjoy things outside of Disney. And look at some of the things available to do! Want to take a helicopter tour of the city? There are several locations in Kissimmee and Orlando that you can pay a few dollars and take that aerial trip you have been longing for! There are skydiving lessons available, fishing excursions, cruises, Universal Studios Orlando Resort with their two theme parks, Legoland, Busch Gardens, Sea World, The Orlando Eye, shopping and dining on I-Drive, outlet malls, wineries, self pick berry farms, dinner theaters, museums and much more! But the point is that Central Florida has so many fun offerings that you should find it virtually impossible to be bored while you stay here.

If you do end up going back home after your program, this is one topic that you will deeply miss. Over half of the former CPs I interviewed each mentioned that they missed going to places like

Jellyrolls (a dueling piano bar on Disney property). This was their after work hangout. They also enjoyed going to Ice Bar on International Drive. Each of them seemed to have chosen places to unwind that didn't include being around their immediate work location. Some of the newer College Program Alumni mentioned Splittsville at Disney Springs. They have discount nights on bowling and amazing food and beverage selections.

#7 You Were Exposed to Various Cultures During Your Program!

This planet is the home to over seven billion people. And within those populated communities, there are millions of different cultures and traditions. Disney prides themselves on Diversity on property and I can say from experience that I have had the pleasure of meeting thousands and thousands of Cast Members over the years that all come from different backgrounds, beliefs and cultures. I learned so much about celebrations and cultures that were not my own that it gave me a greater appreciation for people. You will have probably had the opportunity to try foods that you have never tried before and most likely because your fellow Cast Members have brought it in for a workplace pot luck. Or maybe you did try some of those cultural delights at one of Epcot's events. Either way, congratulations! You broadened your horizons and gave it a chance.

The first Christmas season I worked at Walt Disney World, I learned about the holiday: Noche Buena. Noche Buena is a Latin Holiday celebrated on December 24th. Others celebrate it as Christmas Eve but in the Latin community, it is about family and food and celebrating with loved ones. In almost every photo my Cast had shown me, a roasted whole pig was the centerpiece of the feast. The point is that I wasn't aware of such a celebration until I began working with others with very diverse backgrounds and cultures.

#6 You Were Able to Get Into the Parks For Free!

Did someone say free admission into the theme parks at Disney? Yes! This is truly one of the best perks available to Cast Members! Just look at current ticket prices. With a single day, single park ticket costing over a hundred dollars, your Cast ID and Maingate has given you the ability to park hop throughout the day. The value of this adds up quickly each time you go play in the parks. Hopefully you never complained about the long lines though. Since you have the ability to go to the parks when you want, you should not complain about the lines. Don't forget that there are people in line who have saved for a lifetime to go to these parks only once. So what that you couldn't ride Haunted Mansion three times today! You can always come back another day and try again. Enjoy this benefit! You will miss it once your program ends. I promise you that this is true. Everyone has a favorite ride or maybe a favorite in each of the parks. And it is an amazing feeling to bring a change of clothes with you to work, work your shift, change and then head over to the parks. Or even the reverse of that. Head to the parks, play some and then head out for work with plenty of time to spare. There is truly no other place like this in the world! When I was an hourly Cast Member, I would have to refrain from buying a turkey leg if I was playing in the park before work. I would feel tired from eating that gigantic turkey leg before going to work. This is never a good plan for me.

#5 Your Networking Could Lead to a Long Term Career!

At some point or another have you given some type of thought to want you want to do for a career. At least, I hope you have. Even if you constantly change you major field of study at school, you are still thinking about what you want to do for a living. So while on your College Program, you kept your record card clean and watched your attendance carefully. You partnered with your leadership team and they even referred you to meet with other leaders to help get your name out there. You have applied to a position or two that was available on the career website with the blessing of your leadership team. Great! Maybe you will be able to grab that dream role after all! But don't count out any of the Cast Members you just met! Some of them will be going back to school or maybe even go onto work for other companies. You never know where your next career opportunity will come from! You should make it a habit to keep in touch with these people. Maybe one of them or maybe even you start your own company! You have the potential to recruit or be recruited from this situation if you kept in touch and had a good working relationship. Never count out an opportunity. Never burn a bridge, so to speak. Taking your network for granted will backfire on you almost every time. I have seen former CPs recruit their coworkers for other companies in the past.

When there are special events available to work, these are also fantastic opportunities to grow your network. Some of these opportunities present themselves as extra hours on the HUB while others require Cast Members to sign up on posted flyers in your work area. I had mentioned previously that occasionally extra hours could come up in the form of parade access control (PAC) shifts which would allow you to help with crowd control, information assistance and assisting areas with stroller parking. These shifts pop up when special events take place and are snatched up quickly. Besides these special hard ticket events, there are other times that specifically come to mind when I have seen College Program Cast chosen to work outside their normal area.

Star Wars Weekends, Epcot's Flower and Garden Festival and their Food and Wine Festival are special events that post flyers in the various work areas across property. These events look for Cast from Merchandise, Food and Beverage and sometimes Operations to help build their temporary rosters with eager Cast. Working these events are great since you can meet new people, grow your networking base, gain new experiences and add them to your resume. If your attendance is excellent and you have support from your leadership team, you should absolutely give this opportunity a chance!

#4 Your Internship Was at the Busiest Vacation Destination in the World!

You've seen the crowds. Every year the parks get busier and busier. You have been playing in the parks and have been a part of the crowds. The parks become busy and it almost doesn't matter what time of the year. You thought that the early year would be calm and quiet? Think again, marathons are happening and suddenly the resorts and parks are filled with people wearing racing medals. Oh maybe Easter is slow? Maybe the days after but depending on when Easter falls, Star Wars Weekends are near and the parks are busy again. But you still need to give yourself a huge pat on the back! You have successfully completed your paid internship at the busiest vacation destination in the world. If you can conquer this program, you should be able to handle yourself out in the "real world". And you also chose to do an internship that was paid with room and board available as opposed to the non-paid internships that you could have busted your backside over and still had to find a place to live on your own and had no guarantee of landing a paying career out of it as well.

#3 The Skills You Have Learned Will Stay With You!

Having and enhancing your skill set while you learn is helpful when it comes time to market yourself for a career. Not to mention that adding to your skills helps mold your abilities and character over time. We've mentioned safety before but what about other nuances? What other skills have you acquired or enhanced? Take a moment and think about that. What are you doing now that you might not have been doing before in your pre-College Program life? You learned that Cast are taught to point using either a two fingered point or using your entire hand to point. Some cultures find a single finger point offensive or threatening no matter which finger is used. You have now been doing this Disney Point so much that this habit will most likely stick with you through the remainder of your days.

Next, look at how many times people have approached you with questions. You had questions thrown your way at work every day. Some of them were repetitive and a few were unique that surprised you each day. But you learned quickly that it is best to listen to the entire question before getting ahead of yourself with a potentially wrong answer. Especially if you made the mistake of cutting the Guest's question off with your answer before they finished. Your listening skills are definitely enhanced. You now take an extra second to process what you are being asked and delivering your legendary Guest Service.

Look at your new money saving skills! You now know how to make your dollars stretch! Remember all of those times I repetitively hassled you about setting a budget and sticking to it? Having and maintaining a budget is a huge step in being a responsible adult. Not everyone has unlimited resources or a deep pocket trust fund. Think of this new budgeting skill as your step into true independence! It is a great feeling to have knowing that you are able to take care of yourself. And you have done a marvelous job up until now so way to go!

#2 Your College Program Experience Looks Great on Your Resume!

Maybe you didn't give much thought to your resume because you were having too much fun? Maybe you didn't think that your handful of months would have that much of an impact on your resume? But the fact is that working for Disney (if even only as a College Program Cast Member) does look fantastic on your resume. Having your Disney College Program on your working resume is very impressive to companies. After I left, I was courted by a few companies and was quite surprised as to just how much they were eager to want me to join them because of my extensive Disney experience. Ultimately, I chose to work for myself as a writer. And I'm not just referring to this book but I am also an author of two sci/fi fantasy novels and novellas. I am also writing some travel articles for various publications as well. With the successful completion of your program, do not count out your experience with Disney. And if you decide to pursue a Professional Internship, you then have more opportunities to to network and grow if you decide to pursue a long term Disney career! By the end of your program you have probably made several trips into Disney University and have seen the service award statues in the cases. At one point all of us have dreamed about reaching at least the twenty fifth anniversary statue. Just make sure that you do take advantage of the resume writing classes that are offered on property to Cast Members. You should consider actually writing two types of resumes: a Disney specific resume and a Real World resume.

A Disney specific resume is a type of resume that highlights your performance with the company as a Cast Member. You want this kind of resume if you have any plans whatsoever to pursue a career with Disney. So your resume doesn't need to include what a typical resume would include like: used a register to ring up Guests or cleaned restrooms. The company knows what your previous Disney job title and description looks like. What they are looking for is your ability to articulate how you incorporated the Four Key Basics into your role, how did you support your team overall and what accomplishments or projects did you complete during your program? These are important benchmarks that help set you apart from the other candidates applying for Disney roles. Your network will also be a valuable asset in preparing this type of resume.

The Real World resume is not referring to an application to try out for the MTV reality television series by the same namesake. It is referring to building a solid technical resume that you will want to use to pursue a position with any non-Disney company. This one will require you to cover the same topics as a Disney resume but also to be able to show off what technical skills you have that would be a valuable asset for any potential employer. This resume should not have more than a page or page and a half of information. Don't forget to include your educational experience! Remember: Most employers are looking for your educational achievement as a part of their basic qualifications for the position you are applying for.

#1 The Friendships You Make Here Will Last a Lifetime!

Your roommates (assuming you all got along) have helped make you feel at home in your apartment. They have, in effect, become a part of your family. They have helped you through any tough times including being homesick. You have all built each other up when one of you are down. They have become a true definition of family for you. Your work area has embraced you and you have enjoyed working with them. Maybe there were CPs in other apartments or locations that you just met randomly and have boded with. Maybe you have even met a significant other and have been in a relationship during your program. Whatever your scenario(s) is, you will miss these people when you leave. And they will miss you as well. The beautiful thing about everyone carrying smartphones or using social media apps, it is much easier now to keep in touch with your former roommates and coworkers than ever before. Take a look back to the College Programs back in 2002 or earlier. Most of these apps and types of phones weren't available to everyone. So keeping in contact was much more daunting. You would have to call long distance and incur long distance charges. You could send a "snail" mail letter but it took several days to arrive and if they responded, their response could take weeks. Could you send a text message? sure a lot of phones had that ability but it used to cost per text message and that would add up quick. You will want to take as many photos of the people who you were close with because it is still fun to this day to go back and look at those memories even ten years after originally taking them. And all of you have something big in common that you do not have with the friends of yours back home: you all worked in the Happiest Place on Earth at one point in your lives. To this day, I am still friends with hundreds of my former Cast Members and peers. Some of these Cast Members were Full Time, Part Time, Seasonal and College Program Cast Members. Not everyone will have the opportunity to be involved with the Disney College Program. So again, congratulations on a successful program and a job well done!

Chapter 16
A Final Few Words

So here we are. And now you are nearing the end of the book. And again, I apologize for how repetitive much of the subject matter was in the content. The point of being repetitive is to condition you for your program. Well you have heard a lot of information about things and behaviors to avoid. You have heard many different ways on how your program can come to an unsuccessful screeching halt. You have also read about how others actions can affect you as well as how you have a direct impact on the overall experience. But do you still feel like this is overwhelming? You shouldn't. I absolutely and wholeheartedly believe in the Disney College Program. This internship is more valuable to you than you realize. I chose to repeat some information just in the hopes that you will understand that all of the pitfalls are completely avoidable.

Even though much of the warnings in this book appear to be common sense or things that you knew existed, sometimes it is just helpful to have this information reinforced for you. You are no longer able to say that you didn't know or understand. But in spite of the warnings of what to do and what not to do, you still have freedom of choice. Just always keep in the back of your mind this last piece of advice: for every choice, there is an action and a reaction. And how they play out are based solely on how you choose.

"How did you manage to compile this information?" you might ask. Well as I stated in the beginning of the book, I have interviewed hundreds of College Program Cast Members over my eleven and a half years outside of work. So as does the information span well over a decade, the subject matter and answers are timeless in their ability to guide you. I am also including a real sample of the questions and a set of honest responses from one former College Program Cast Member in this chapter!

The questionnaire with responses comes from Patricia from New England:

1) Besides close friends or family who are CP Alumni, did your school have a recruiting session for the DCP? If so, what kind of presentation did they give you?

"So actually my school didn't have any kind of presentation for DCP. Supposedly there was some kind of tour schedule for an information session but it only happened once the entire 3 years I was attending. The only frequent reminder about the program were little things like table toppers or ads on the school tv but that was literally it."

2) I understand that there is verbal interview over the phone and a computerized written test (or personality test) is administered at some point. Was the personality test lengthy?

"I don't remember the test being lengthy. Once you got the hang of what kind of answers they wanted you moved through it pretty fast. It was like 10-15 minutes."

3) Was there anything about your program that you feel should have been presented to you ahead of time so you could be better prepared?

"Not so much - at least in a work related sense. I mean there's plenty of kids who go who underestimate the hours and the lifestyle and being on their own but otherwise you're pretty much told anything you're meant to know. Though I might've also had an advantage from knowing about (a family members) program."

4) Do you feel that you had networking opportunities on your program to help you if you wanted to further your career?

"I certainly think so. I mean that's one of the main reasons people go is for resume and network building. I loved my leads and I think they'd gladly help with any job opportunities I had. It might be more advantageous within Disney itself for me if I ever decide to go back but it is always a wow factor of conversation starter whenever somebody sees it"

5) What do you NOT miss about the program?

"there's nothing about the program itself that I don't miss. I was lucky in what location I was in so anything that I don't miss a year later, are things that are personal preference outside the program itself. Like the weather or the really touristy towns or even some of my roommates lol. "

6) What do you miss the most?

"next to my coworkers and leaders who while I still have them on fb (Facebook), I really do miss cause they're probably my favorite people I've ever worked for/with, I think I miss just being in the parks itself more than anything. Like being able to just go walk around n hang out. There's always little things that remind me of it that always gets me a little bummed out. Yea the free transport was pretty sweet too, and also the nicest/biggest apartment I've ever lived in but it's still just being AT the parks"

7) If you did a second program, what would you do differently and why?

"first off I think I would actually want to do Disneyland instead of world. I had kind of wanted to do that more in the first place but they didn't have housing, though I've heard that's changed now. Plus from what I've seen and heard from articles, videos, and cps from Cali, (Disney)land just seems to understand what the experience is supposed to be about more than world. Though I know there's a lot of factors that play into why that is but nevertheless. I also would not do 6 roommates again. 1-3 tops. It's just too many people to be together and it creates unnecessary stress and drama. The only positive is that it's a little cheaper. But I'll pay more to keep my sanity."

8) Do any of the skills you learned carry over into your non-Disney life now?

"Aside from the fact that I'll never be able to NOT do the Disney point ever again I think my speed and efficiency really improved from being at the lodge as well as my multitasking. And I think the most prominent thing I gained from working with such nice people is that I can actually be myself at my jobs now because of It. Before I was always sheltering my opinion or dealing with crappy coworkers cause I felt I had to but now having had a taste of an actually enjoyable job, it was kind of like "screw it. What you see is what you get." And that was huge. So even though it's not really a skill, that's the biggest effect it had on me."

I chose this one questionnaire to post due to its balanced blend of answers and also to give you, the reader, an idea of how some of this advice was compiled.

And finally, please remember to embrace the fun during your college program and embrace it responsibly. Yes, this is a work environment. And yes, you are required to work. But there are not many companies in the big beautiful world that allow you to have fun while you work. There will be plenty of time to play. You will not be working every waking moment of your program. Nobody can keep up that pace and maintain their physical and mental health. Make your friends. Take your photos. Play in the parks and enjoy being in an exclusive alumni that not everyone in the world will be a part of. Be the best Cast Member...no. Be the best person you can be while deciding on what you will be doing for your future career! This isn't really the end of your program but just one of many steps in the real beginning of your journey through life. I wish you the best in all of your future endeavors.

Bonus
Further Support

I thank you again for taking the time to purchase this book. It has been a pleasure for me to compile this information for the purpose of helping be your unofficial guide through your College Program. I know it wasn't exactly all pixie dust and everything is perfect. Instead, I do hope you found this it to be a strong and realistic resource to help guide you through your Disney College Program. But I do recognize that with such a lack of information on the internet, not everything may have been clarified for you. Is there something that you didn't see in this book that you are still wondering about? Maybe you were looking for further clarification on a topic covered? I do believe in the College Program whole heartedly and want to see you finish this program successfully! So don't hesitate to reach out to me for further guidance. Feel free to reach out to me via email:
TELLMEMORECPGUIDE@OUTLOOK.COM

When sending your correspondence, please include the following in the body of your email:

- Your First and Last name
- Where and When you purchased this book or e-book.
- When your program is scheduled to start.
- Your hometown or school you are attending.
- Your question.
- Also, specify whether you are interested in learning more about my other writings and literary works, I will be happy to add you to my mailing list if you do.

I will do the best I can to assist you. It may take me a day or two to respond back initially but I will respond. Please understand that I can only give you information on things that are NOT considered: Proprietary Information like trade secrets, unpublished policies and park capacities as an example. I will respond back in any case and explain if there is a reason why I cannot release certain types of information. Remember, when you sign up to be a Cast Member, everyone signs a non-disclosure agreement. And I have absolutely no interest on breaching that agreement. I know I am not interested in any legal issues and neither is my publisher.

So don't be afraid to send me an email with your questions or even send an email letting me know you survived your Disney College Program! And most of all, best of luck to you!

About the Author

Eric Root was originally from San Jose, CA but has had the pleasure of living in Oregon, Washington, Massachusetts and Florida. He has held various retail management positions for the following companies: Pro Image, Print Plus, Aaron Brothers Art & Framing, Mars Incorporated, The Disney Store and at Walt Disney World. His total experience as a leader in business is over fifteen years combined. His passions in business include: Recognition, Career Pathing, Subordinate Development and Communication.

He has enjoyed being creative over the years with drawing, photography and writing. He has been writing since 2009. And under the pen name: E. R. Root, Eric currently has two published sci fi / fantasy novels: The Carpenter's Daughter and The Nine Elements. He also has two novellas (short story or half novels): Princess Marissa and Her Missing Prince, Legend of the Huntress: A Corsair Tale. He is currently working on a third book in this series as well. Under the same pen name, Eric is actively writing travel stories which are in the works for various online publications. He currently resides in Central Florida and is looking to further his writing in the field of travel. In his spare time, he collects older action figures and comics.

Sources

Published STCU Disney Full Time Union Collective Bargaining Agreement Contract:

http://www.uniteherelocal362.org/wp-content/uploads/FINAL-2014-FT-STCU-CBA-2.pdf

The Disney College Program Website:

http://cp.disneycareers.com/en/default/

Disney Character Audition Info:

https://disneyprogramsblog.com/disney-college-program-auditions/

Published Disney Look Guidelines:

cdn.disneycareers.com/managed/DisneyLookBook3_7_FINAL.pdf

Article from the Orlando Sentinel Regarding Disney College Program Applicants:

http://www.orlandosentinel.com/business/tourism/os-disney-college-program-20150130-story.html

And a special thank you goes out to the hundreds of

former College Program Cast Members that contributed to this guide.

You may not have had the information you needed when you started.

But take comfort in knowing that future CPs will!

CPSIA information can be obtained
at www.ICGtesting.com
Printed in the USA
FSOW03n1313051216
28194FS